MW01119676

# Mobile Professional Voluntarism and International Development

Helen Louise Ackers • James Ackers-Johnson

# Mobile Professional Voluntarism and International Development

## Killing Me Softly?

palgrave
macmillan

Helen Louise Ackers
University of Salford
Salford, United Kingdom

James Ackers-Johnson
University of Salford
Salford, United Kingdom

This Palgrave Pivot imprint is published by Springer Nature
The registered company is Nature America Inc.
The registered company address is: 1 New York Plaza, New York, NY 10004, U.S.A.

*We dedicate our book to the mothers and mothers-to-be of Uganda*

# FOREWORD

I believe we are entering a time when traditional approaches to overseas aid are giving way to new forms of development, involving new sources of finance and new partnerships. In this context, the health partnership model is increasingly relevant. It enables countries to work more collaboratively and at scale. It is an approach that is grounded in the powerful transformative concepts of mutual benefit of co-development and co-learning, themes central to this book – and to the Sustainable Development Goals which now shape our work.

The Health Partnership Scheme, funded by Department for International Development (DFID) and managed by Tropical Health and Education Trust (THET), has provided 50,000 training courses or other educational opportunities to developing-country health workers with over 60,000 UK health professional days spent volunteering. And so my interest was suitably piqued by the title of Chapter 3 of this book, 'Fetishising and commodifying "training?"'. I couldn't resist and neither should you.

I expect readers, especially those with experience in health partnerships, will find this book challenging and important. Its frankness and willingness to take on big issues and suggest possible solutions is refreshing, and while I wouldn't agree with all of its arguments or recommendations – and knowing the authors they would be frankly disappointed if I were to do so – this is a book to be engaged with.

We are not convinced, for example, that the authors are right in generalising from their experiences in the Sustainable Volunteering Project (SVP) to draw conclusions about the health partnership model. From our perspective, the SVP is one (albeit, very interesting) project amongst 200 that were funded by DFID. Some of the challenges encountered in the SVP have been fully addressed by other projects, such as the management of trainees' expectations of per diem payments. We also have more sympathy, as you might expect, with the need for DFID ministers to communicate clearly with the UK public. This necessitates a simplification of messages, with some implications for evaluation. This is amply balanced in our experience, with an appetite for nuance and learning at DFID.

The case studies in Chapter 5 are to be savoured. Based on the notion that you've got to fail in order to learn – an idea, incidentally, highly valued by THET as well – they provide a wonderfully detailed and valuable portrait of the challenges encountered by practitioners on the ground.

This book pulls no punches, and with a style both academic and personal the authors challenge us all to put our collective shoulder to the wheel to develop a more structured approach to professional volunteer deployment within health partnerships based on principles of negotiated conditionality. This is to be not only applauded but also acted upon for, as the book quite rightly argues, this way leads towards evidence-based incremental systems change.

The wide-ranging critique of aid, based on the authors' years of experience of managing programmes of work in Uganda, covers a great deal of ground examining the nature of development interventions, ethical standards in volunteer deployment as well as the efficacy of donations or the meaningfulness of prevailing evaluation methodologies. It also has a lot to say about the tough issues faced on the ground by health professionals working in development, such as corruption and labour substitution.

The challenges thrown down by this book, based on first-hand experience, are vital in helping us understand better the nature of the solutions. As we join together to co-create a better world I warmly welcome this book's important contribution.

Tropical Health and Education Trust

Ben Simms
Chief Executive

# ACKNOWLEDGEMENTS

We would like to acknowledge the support, both financial and personal, that we have received from the Tropical Health and Education Trust, which made the Sustainable Volunteering Project (SVP) possible.[1] As volunteer manager, Graeme Chisholm has remained a close colleague always willing to discuss ideas. We are also very grateful to our fellow trustees in the Liverpool-Mulago Partnership, particularly the Chair, Mrs Vanessa Harris, who have extended their commitment, support and trust. Our colleagues in the Ugandan Maternal and Newborn Hub, especially Sarah Hoyle, Robert Bates and Helen Allott, have provided ongoing support and advice and we have learnt a huge amount from them.

We would also like to acknowledge the vision and support of our current employer and colleagues at the University of Salford, UK. Whilst many of us find the title of our School something of a mouthful, the multi-disciplinary and multi-professional character of the School of Nursing, Midwifery, Social Work and Social Science has created a fertile and supportive environment for this highly complex and time-consuming action-oriented intervention.

The past 8 years have been challenging and, at times, extremely frustrating, but ultimately very exciting. We have been working at the boundaries and intersections of knowledge. We have gained significantly, both intellectually and personally, from our relationships with the SVP volunteers. The UK and the NHS in particular should feel extremely proud of the professionals it has nurtured and the high levels of professionalism, compassion, innovation and commitment they demonstrate. They have played a key role not only within the frame of their own disciplines but also as critical knowledge brokers, action-researchers and team players.

Finally, and most importantly, we would like to extend our sincere thanks to those Ugandan health workers who have become our colleagues and friends over the years. The context within which they are attempting to exercise professional responsibility and clinical excellence is punishing to say the least, and their ability to imagine a better reality, in which public services can be improved and mothers' and babies' lives saved, is challenged on a daily basis. Our conclusion, that development aid through professional voluntarism is largely failing to translate into sustainable systems change, in no way reflects on their capabilities or individual commitment. We would like to be able to name those of you who have played such a critical role in supporting the Sustainable Volunteering Project and ongoing work but we are aware that doing so may have damaging personal repercussions. You know who you are and we thank you. We hope that the honesty and trust that you have shown, and we have presented here, will generate new evidence-based opportunities for international professional relationships focused on systems change in the Ugandan Public Health Sector.

## NOTE

1. The Sustainable Volunteering Project (SVP) is funded by the Tropical Health and Education Trust (THET) as part of the Health Partnership Scheme, which is supported by the UK Department for International Development (DFID). The views expressed are those of the authors and do not necessarily reflect the views of THET.

# CONTENTS

# LIST OF FIGURES

# LIST OF TABLES

# CHAPTER 1

# Mobile Professional Voluntarism and International Development 'Aid'

**Abstract** Chapter 1 sets the research on which this book is based in context. It discusses the relationship that Aid has with concepts of equality and poverty, and distinguishes humanitarian (emergency) relief contexts from those focused on capacity building. It also questions the efficacy of Aid and raises the possibility that Aid itself may have damaging consequences. Moving from Aid to the wider concept of 'global health', the chapter discusses the role that forms of highly skilled migration, such as professional voluntarism, can play in capacity building. Finally, it discusses the methodological approach taken in this action-research study.

**Keywords** AID · International development · Professional voluntarism · Action-research

## INTRODUCTION

This book reports on our experiences of managing and researching the deployment of professionals employed in the UK, primarily but not exclusively in the National Health Service (NHS), to public health facilities in Uganda.[1] The authors have been involved in interventions focused on improving maternal and newborn health in Uganda for the past 7 years through the work of a British charity known as the Liverpool-Mulago-Partnership (LMP[2]). LMP is one of many health partnerships active in Uganda and linked, in recent years, under the umbrella of the Ugandan

© The Author(s) 2017
H.L. Ackers, J. Ackers-Johnson, *Mobile Professional Voluntarism and International Development*, DOI 10.1057/978-1-137-55833-6_1

Maternal and Newborn Hub.[3] In 2012, LMP received funding from the Tropical Health and Education Trust for the 'Sustainable Volunteering Project' (SVP). The 'SVP' was funded in the first instance for 3 years, during which time it deployed around 50 long-term and many more short-term volunteers. The whole project has been subject to intense ongoing evaluation focused both on volunteer learning and the returns to the NHS[4] and on the impact on hosting Ugandan healthcare facilities and health workers. This book focuses on the second dimension capturing the impacts of these kinds of intervention on the receiving/hosting country or the 'development' perspective.

Whilst the work is deeply and necessarily contextualised, the results create important opportunities for knowledge transfer and lesson learning in other fields of health and social policy and in other low- and medium-income countries.

## DEVELOPMENT, AID AND INEQUALITY

Countries, such as Uganda, are often described either as 'developing' (in contrast to the 'developed') or, more recently, as 'lower- and middle-income countries' (LMICs) in contrast to high-income or resource-rich economies. This characterisation suggests binaries: the 'haves' and 'have nots' or at least a continuum from high to low resource. Of course, you may have high-income economies (such as the USA or the emerging economies of India and China) with very high and increasing levels of absolute poverty and inequality. Even 'low-income' economies such as Uganda provide a comfortable and lucrative home to many very rich and highly cosmopolitan people with access to high-quality private health facilities both at home and across the world.

The complexity and relative character of inequality and its spatial dynamics are somewhat lost in this characterisation of 'international development'. The project we are reporting on is focused on the *public* health system in Uganda and, more specifically, on the delivery of services to those Ugandan people whose only claim to health care is on the basis of their citizenship. Or, put differently, those citizens who lack the income to access a wide range of other options. In Uganda (as in India or in the USA), health status is related directly to ability to pay; the more money you have the higher your opportunities. Only those with no other options will turn to the residualised 'safety net', that is, the public health system. Perhaps the only factor distinguishing a country like Uganda from other countries is the fact that this is the case for a majority of its population and countries such as the USA (or China and India) have the resources, if not the political will, to significantly reduce health inequalities.

According to published data, Uganda has one of the highest levels of maternal mortality in the world. The Ugandan Ministry of Health's Strategic Plan suggests that little, if any, progress has been made in terms of improvements in Maternal Health (Millennium Development Goal 5) and, more specifically, in reducing maternal mortality (MOH 2010: 43). A United Nations report on the MDGs describes Uganda's progress as 'stagnant' (UNDP 2013: iii). Figures on maternal mortality in Uganda vary considerably depending on the source. The World Health Organisation reports maternal mortality ratios (MMRs) of 550 per 100,000 live births (WHO 2010).[5] However, the benchmarking exercise undertaken as part of the Sustainable Volunteering Project (McKay and Ackers 2013: 23) indicated wide variation between facilities in MMRs reported to the Ministry of Health. Perhaps of greater significance, it reiterated the very poor quality of reporting and records management resulting in significant underreporting. The figures for Hoima Regional Referral Hospital likely reflect improvements in records management following the intervention of a UK Health Partnership (the Hoima-Basingstoke Health Partnership) rather than a greater incidence of mortality. Indeed, more detailed audit of case files by an SVP volunteer indicated levels in Mbale regional referral hospital of over 1000 (more than double reported levels) (Fig. 1.1).[6]

These figures are shocking indeed. However, it is important not to gain the impression that all women in Uganda face an equal prospect of dying in childbirth. Data collected from the private ward in Mulago National Referral Hospital paint quite a different picture with only one maternal death recorded between January 2011 and October 2012 compared to 183 deaths on the public ward. Interestingly, the caesarean section rate on the private ward is more than double that on the main public ward (51.6% compared to 25.4%) (Ackers 2013: 23). Inter-sectoral inequalities within the country are as alarming as inter-country comparisons. And, in case of Mulago Hospital, the health care staff treating patients on the private ward are exactly the same as those on the public ward.[7]

The simple but important point we are trying to make at the outset is that the context within which the Sustainable Volunteering Project is deploying volunteers is best described as one of profound social

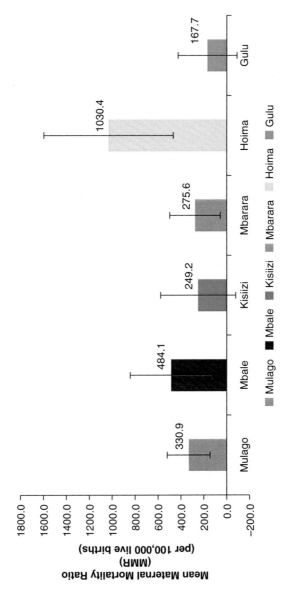

**Fig. 1.1**   Mean maternal mortality ratios by facility, Uganda, 2011–2012 (*Source:* Ackers (2013))

inequality rather than poverty per se. And, the 'low-resource setting' we refer to in this book is the public healthcare system in Uganda and not Uganda or Ugandan health care, as a whole.

One of the problems with the popular use of the word 'poverty', or even more so, 'the poor', is that they infer the kind of passivity displayed in media fund-raising campaigns with images of human 'victims' needing 'help' splashed across posters and television screens. And, the corollary of this is, of course, the 'helpers' or good-doers who dip into their pockets. This 'donor–recipient' model of development AID continues to taint international relationships. It is convenient and valuable to distinguish at this juncture two forms of intervention or perhaps, to avoid caricature, two contexts. Bolton suggests that, 'broadly speaking, AID can have two aims. It either provides humanitarian relief in response to emergencies, or it tries to stimulate longer-term development' (2007: 75). Humanitarian or emergency AID then seeks to provide an immediate response to catastrophic events such as famine, earthquakes or wars. In such situations, immediate service intervention is easier to justify and concerns around unintended consequences or collateral damage less pressing. This type of activity could, in theory and out of necessity, be achieved by foreign volunteers in the absence of local staff. The deployment of 'Mercy Ships,' for example, is designed to 'fill the gaps in health care systems' through service delivery.[8] And emergency AID may be provided in any context without in-depth analysis of a country's economic status or political decision making.

Bolton calculates that around 95 % of AID falls into the alternative category of 'development aid' – a form of investment which is both 'much better value' (in terms of promoting resilience) and 'harder to get right' (2007: 76). This AID comes from a diversity of sources including, as Bolton indicates, charitable donations and philanthropy (of which a sizeable component are linked to religious organisations pursuing their own agendas); National AID provided by governments and International AID provided by organisations such as the World Bank and the United Nations. The boundaries between these forms of AID are fuzzy and the political imperatives (underlying national and international AID and its links with diplomacy and trade) combined with the marketing functions of charitable fund-raisers together result in an opaqueness and lack of honesty about impacts. Bolton argues that the pressure to raise funds results in a tendency to simplify and exaggerate the effectiveness of AID and concludes that, 'the outcome is probably the most unaccountable multi-billion dollar industry in the world' (p. 79).

To put AID in perspective, the Ugandan Ministry of Health published figures indicating an annual spend of 1281.14 billion shillings (about £156.5 million). Of this, 68 % (£150 million) is provided by the Ugandan government and 32 % (£106.5 million) by 'donors'. The growth in donor share is quite alarming, almost doubling from 13.7 % in 2011 (MOH 2015). Department for International Development (DFID) figures for 2015 indicate a spend of over £26 million in 2014/2015 on health in Uganda; the majority of which (63 %) goes on reproductive and maternal and newborn health (DFID 2011). These figures are indicative only and most certainly under-estimate the monetary value of AID, reflecting only the direct inter-governmental funding that travels down through the Ministry.[9] Health Partnerships are largely funded as local charities, and whilst the amount of money involved may be quite high, this is dwarfed by the real costs of in-kind contributions through volunteer labour.

Moyo's book, with its stark and 'incendiary'[10] title, *Dead Aid* (sub-titled: *Why AID is not working and how there is another way for Africa*), had a major impact on the design of the SVP. Moyo argues that the culture of AID derives from 'the liberal sensibility that the rich should help the poor and that the form of this help should be Aid' (p. xix). With reference to its impact on 'systemic poverty' (as opposed to humanitarian crises), Moyo concludes that AID has been and continues to be 'an unmitigated political, economic and humanitarian disaster for most parts of the developing world' (2009: xix). She goes beyond many other writers who express similar concern at the efficacy of AID to contend that AID is not only ineffectual but, of far greater concern, it also generates externality effects that actually cause damage. AID is 'consumed' rather than invested:

> Were AID simply innocuous – just not doing what it claimed it would do – this book would not have been written. The problem is that AID is not benign – it's malignant. No longer part of the potential solution, it's part of the problem – in fact, AID is the problem. (p. 47)

AID has been described as an 'industry' by actors in high-income (donor) settings; it is also seen very much as an industry in low-resource settings. Indeed, poverty is a magnet for AID and the more overtly poor and destitute the case, the greater the prospect of attracting investment.

Sadly, in the Ugandan context, this creates a vested interest for local leaders in the deliberate preservation and presentation of impoverishment and chaos in order to suck in cash and create opportunities for embezzlement. In that sense, poverty is both functional and profitable.

## FROM 'AID' TO GLOBAL HEALTH

These kinds of anxieties, about the effectiveness of AID, fuelled by political correctness about the use of the term 'development' have led to new concepts to capture the investment dimension and focus on longer-term systemic change. The Tropical Health and Education Trust is one of a growing number of intermediaries funded by the UK's DFID and focusing on 'capacity building' and 'sustainability'. Locating itself within the 'global health' agenda, THET describes its mission as building long-term resilient health systems to promote improved access to essential health care as a basic human right (THET 2015). At the centre of this strategy is the concept of 'human resources for health' or 'HRH'.

The global health agenda has usefully shifted attention from the haves–have nots and donor–recipient binaries referred to before, talking instead, somewhat hopefully, of partnerships and 'win–win' relationships. Lord (Nigel) Crisp has pushed this agenda forward arguing quite forcefully that the UK's National Health Service has as much to learn from low-resource settings as vice versa. Focusing again on health systems (rather than poor people per se), Crisp suggests that the concept of global health 'embraces everything that we share in health terms globally' (2010: 9). Crisp's approach rest on two ideas. First, that health systems in high-resource settings are facing (growing) challenges in terms of resources and sustainability and, second, that globalisation is itself creating complex mobilities (both human and microbial) and interdependencies that effectively challenge the autonomy and resilience of nation states: we are all increasingly connected, whether we like it or not. The growing mobility of health workers or the spread of Ebola are prime examples. It is interesting also to see how Crisp and THET have started to slip the word 'innovation' alongside development, although they shy away from the language of competition in this fluffy consensual world.

In the context of global health, at least the growing emphasis on human resources has usefully shifted the debate from one about providing 'top-down' cash injections in the form of national or international financial support to (corrupt) governments to supporting forms of knowledge exchange through grounded partnerships.

THET describes its focus on reducing health inequalities in low- and middle-income countries with a particular emphasis on improving access to essential health care (as a basic human right). Achieving this requires significant improvement in health systems and this in turn places the emphasis on human resources:

> The lack of human resources for health is a critical constraint to sustainable development in many lower- and middle-income countries. (THET 2015: 10)

This leads naturally on to what they describe as 'a unique partnership approach that harnesses the skills, knowledge and technical expertise of health professionals to meet the training and education needs identified in low-resource settings'. And 'international volunteering' is one of the key mechanisms it supports to achieve this skills harnessing process.[11]

The Health Partnership Scheme (HPS) managed by THET was launched in 2011 to 'build the capacity of healthcare workers and the faculty needed to train them with a focus on 'lasting improvements to healthcare [ ... ] and service innovation' (THET 2015: 10). The scheme is funded by DFID at a cost of £30 million over 6 years. It is under this scheme and specifically the 'Long-Term Volunteering Programme', that the SVP was funded. THET guidelines set out the following objectives:

HPS Volunteering Grants aim to leverage the knowledge and expertise of UK health professionals by funding efficient, high-quality long-term volunteering programmes linked to development projects. HPS Volunteering Grants should [ ... ] strengthen health systems through building the capacity of human resources for health (THET 2011).

In direct response to these objectives, the SVP set out the following objectives:

- To support evidence-based, holistic and sustainable *systems change* through improved knowledge transfer, translation and impact.
- To promote a more effective, sustainable and mutually beneficial approach to international professional volunteering (as the key *vector of change*).

These goals were then formulated as an action-research question framing the wider intervention:

> To what extent, and under what circumstances, can mobile professional voluntarism promote the kinds of knowledge exchange and translation capable of improving the effectiveness of public health systems in LMICs? (THET 2011)

With these thoughts in mind we designed the SVP evaluation around three potential 'scenarios:'

### Scenario 1: Partial Improvement (Positive Change)

Under this scenario, evidence will indicate that the professional volunteering interventions we are engaging in are at least *partially effective* in promoting systems change. It is important that even this 'partial effect' relates to incremental long-term progress and is not short-lived. Moyo suggests that project evaluations often identify the 'erroneous' impression of AID's success in the shorter term – whilst 'failing to assess long-term sustainability' (2009: 45).

*Policy Implications:* Any positive collateral benefits to individual service recipients (patients), UK volunteers/health systems are to be identified and encouraged.

### Scenario 2: Neutral Impact (No Change)

Under this scenario, evidence will indicate that the professional volunteering interventions we are engaging are generally *neutral* in terms of systems impact. They neither facilitate nor undermine systems change.

*Policy Implications:* Positive outcomes for individual service recipients (patients), volunteers (and the UK), free of unintended consequences, may be identified and supported.

### Scenario 3: Negative Impact (Collateral Damage)

Under this scenario, evidence will indicate that the professional volunteering interventions we are engaging are generally *counter-productive* /damaging in terms of promoting long-term (sustainable) improvements in public health systems.

*Policy Implications:* Any positive gains to individuals (including Ugandan patients) or systems in the UK are tainted with unintended consequences and, on that basis, are unethical and should not be supported.

Our thinking at the time (project commencement) was heavily influenced by concerns expressed about the inadequacy or lack of transparency and honesty in evaluation (Crisp 2007; James et al. 2008: 7; Bolton 2007) and Moyo's powerfully expressed but seemingly ignored assertions about the damaging effects of AID. We were also building on 4 years' direct experience of deploying and managing long-term volunteers.

Interestingly, the literature on the effectiveness of AID (including Moyo's book) rarely if ever refer to the role of human capital investments in the form of 'voluntarism'. Bolton's chapter, 'Pass the Hat Round – Charity Aid', makes various assumptions about what he calls 'Aid's Sunday Drivers' – caricatured as 'amateurs with far too little expertise [ . . . ] who believe all they need to do is turn up and make a difference' (p. 89). Of course, there is some truth behind his concerns about 'foreigners coming from outside' to intervene in people's lives (p. 90). However, his response to his own question, 'is charity capable of providing the help that Africa needs to pull itself out of poverty? Unequivocally, the answer is no' (p. 92) indicates a failure to understand the skills base of many volunteers and the role that volunteers play within organisations (such as health partnerships). Furthermore, it fails to acknowledge the very real monetary value and costs associated with voluntarism and the role that nation states are playing in funding these processes (through intermediaries such as THET). The costs of the HPS scheme (30 million pounds) are dwarfed by the costs to individuals and NHS employers providing cover for released staff. The concept of 'volunteer' tends to detract from the significant economic costs of this form of 'AID'.

These concerns and experiences imposed a huge sense of personal responsibility on us as project managers deploying volunteers. Whilst we could understand the concerns about large volumes of taxpayers' cash being tipped into foreign governments and relate to Moyo's conclusion that this constituted 'Dead Aid' – we were less sure about the effects of voluntarism as AID. The immediate association of voluntarism with altruism, religiosity and 'giving' and the less obvious (but perhaps no less real) relationships with diplomacy and trade lead us to question whether volunteering ultimately had the same effects – hence, the subtitle for our book: 'Killing me Softly?' This is represented in Scenario 3.

## PROFESSIONAL VOLUNTARISM AS HIGHLY SKILLED MIGRATION

We opened this chapter with a discussion about development and AID. Not because this is where we located ourselves as 'experts', but because it is the dominant discourse within which our work is generally situated– and has been funded. Neither of us (as authors) came to this work with backgrounds in international development or global health. Ackers' background as a geographer and social scientist is in highly skilled migration and the role that internationalisation plays in shaping the mobilities of scientists as individuals and scientific capacity. It is interesting to note that the emphasis in this field is more often on the role that the mobility of the highly skilled plays in promoting scientific competitiveness and innovation. The role of human mobility is increasingly recognised as critical to the formulation of the kinds of knowledge relationships that lie at the heart of economic growth. It is important to point out that the processes of international mobility here are by no means unilateral, as is often inferred, echoing the haves (cosmopolitan northern professionals with extensive mobility capital) and have-nots (internationally isolated and parochial) binary. Our research experience suggests that Ugandan health workers and, especially, but not exclusively, doctors have access to very wide and varied international experience. Indeed, it is possible that the (funded) opportunities available to them exceed those open to their peers in the UK.[12] The Ugandan health workforce is surprisingly cosmopolitan and internationally connected especially but not only at senior levels.

Viewed through these disciplinary lenses, both the SVP volunteers and the many Ugandans who have spent time in the UK are first and foremost highly skilled migrants or, if the language of migration is off-putting for some,[13] people exercising forms of professional mobility. The label 'volunteer' (defined simply by the absence of a formal employment relationship or remuneration) does little to capture the motivations of the diverse groups of people involved and has an unfortunate tendency to characterise them, within the donor–recipient model, as 'helpers' (Bolton's Sunday Drivers) or, worse still, in an environment still dominated by religious values, as 'missionaries'. As noted earlier, our research has embraced the motivations, experiences and learning outcomes of volunteers. The findings of this are reported elsewhere (Chatwin et al. 2016). The point here is to consider what added value such volunteers bring to the host society and its public health system.

Ackers-Johnson's background, on the other hand, is in financial and human resource management. The emergence of the HRH agenda in global health immediately demands an understanding of complex human resource dynamics in terms of both ensuring a supply of appropriate 'volunteers' and creating the structures and relationships that support optimal knowledge capture. The Human Resource Management perspective encourages us to view both volunteers and the Ugandan health workers they are engaging with from the perspective of employment quality and career decision making and accentuates commonality rather than difference in human ambitions and the barriers to knowledge mobilisation. It will become clear as the story unfolds that maternal mortality in Uganda is as much about human resource management as it is about clinical skills.

For the purpose of the SVP and this book, we have coined the term 'professional volunteer' to overcome some of our concerns about the (value-laden) concept of volunteer and emphasise the fact that first and foremost the people we are referring to are highly skilled (mobile) professionals. Characterising them as professionals who are engaging in Uganda with fellow professionals (many of whom are also involved in various forms of international mobility) helps us to situate the project within the frame of both international knowledge mobilisation and human resource management. This is the frame within which we have previously engaged in international teams as research collaborators and not as donors. The word 'professional' also hints at motivational dynamics and the fact that, for the majority of 'volunteers', motivation is a complex concept combining altruistic, touristic and career progression components (amongst others).

## RESEARCHING COMPLEX INTERVENTIONS: THE SVP AS ACTION-RESEARCH

Whilst the Crisp report[14] outlines the important potential strategic role of 'Global Health Partnerships' in the 'massive scaling-up of training, education and employment of health workers in developing countries' (Crisp 2007: 2), it also reflects on the very disappointing historical picture with 'any number of well-intentioned initiatives foundering after a few years' (2007: 5). This, argues Crisp, 'leads to a counsel of despair that, despite all the effort over the years, nothing has really changed' (p. 5). He concludes that there has been, 'very little systematic application of knowledge and learning from successful – and failed – projects' (p. 9) and calls for more international studies that, 'show what impact they can make and how they should best be used' (p. 14). The Academy of Medical Royal Colleges' Statement on Volunteering (2013) similarly expresses concern at the quality of evidence on the impacts of volunteering:

> Monitoring and evaluation of volunteering activities does exist but is at present limited. The same is true of research on long-term impacts. There is a pressing need to develop consistent approaches to robust monitoring and evaluation. (p. 2)

And Bolton takes the argument further suggesting that AID organisations (or funding bodies) have a vested interest in showing that AID works:

> Most of the information we get about aid is from charities [who] need to convince us that aid is effective so they can get their hands on our money...most charities simplify and exaggerate how much effect aid can have. (2007: 78)

This echoes common criticisms of evaluation processes conducted in-house and within projects and, as such, tilted in favour of proving that interventions are both necessary and effective. And, most project evaluations in health partnership work are conducted by people who have little if any research experience in the evaluation of complex social processes. The SVP is perhaps somewhat distinct in this respect to the extent that the co-coordinator is an experienced researcher occupying an established academic post, embedded within an active research team, and as such not personally reliant upon the demonstration of project 'success'. Whilst this distance supported a degree of independence and objectivity, the fact that the authors were simultaneously designing, implementing and evaluating the intervention distinguishes the project from classical research. We were not seeking to 'measure' controlled static phenomenon, and reduce 'contamination' to a minimum (MRC 2008), but rather to institute change processes and capture their impacts longitudinally.

The emphasis on change processes in a program such as the SVP, coupled with the paucity of reliable secondary data, demanded an innovative and iterative multi-method approach. Building on many years' experience of research on highly skilled mobilities and knowledge transfer processes, the evaluation strategy embraced a range of methods complementing and balancing each other through the process of triangulation (Iyer et al. 2013). As researchers, we were acutely aware at the outset of the limitations of facility-generated secondary data. Accurate, reliable data on maternal and newborn health simply do not exist in Uganda. We therefore conducted a major benchmarking exercise across the ten HUB facilities (including health centres and hospitals). This was an interactive process in itself and was as much about improving data collection and record keeping as it was about data capture; indeed, the process included training of record keeping staff. These data should be regarded with caution (as noted earlier).[15] As Gilson et al. note (2011), even in this 'hard data' context there is no single reality, no simple set of undisturbed facts and the data that we do see are essentially socially constructs.

The project has also used simple before-and-after testing schemes using Likert scales to assess learning and skills enhancement during formal training programmes. Capturing the impacts of volunteer engagement on health workers – and more specifically on behaviour and systems change – is far more complex. We have utilised a range of measures including qualitative interviewing of volunteers, structured monthly reporting schedule for all volunteers and bi-annual workshops. Wherever possible, volunteers have been interviewed at least three times (depending on their length of stay with interviews prior to, during and post-return). We have over 150[16] verbatim transcripts drawn from all 10 HUB locations. Most of these have been conducted face to face in Uganda or the UK with some taking place via Skype. Where appropriate, email has also been used to discuss issues.

The research has also involved interviews and focus groups with Ugandan health workers, line managers and policy makers (about 50 to date).[17] The authors have also spent many months in Ugandan health facilities and working with Uganda health workers in the UK. The project coordinator and manager each makes regular visits (around four per year) ranging from 2 weeks to 5 months in duration and we have deployed two social scientists as long-term volunteers embedded within the SVP. This intense ethnographic work is recorded in project notes and diaries and is perhaps the most insightful of all of our methods. The qualitative material has been coded into a software package for qualitative analysis (NVIVO10) and subjected to inductive thematic analysis.[18]

In addition to this, volunteers have been encouraged, where appropriate, to develop specific audits to support contextualisation and highly focused interventions. This has included audits on, for example, maternal deaths, triage and early warning scoring systems, antibiotic use and C-section rates. These audits are small scale and necessarily inherit the same problems with the accuracy of data and of medical records as the wider study.

We have described the study as an example of action-research. It is necessarily iterative and as such we did not set out to achieve a specific sample size or end point but continue to spend time in Uganda interviewing and observing work in public health facilities and facilitating active workshops to encourage discussion around key issues.[19] Indeed, it is through this iterative process that we have come to identify the challenges that we believe are central to understanding both resistance to change in Ugandan health systems and the efficacy of professional voluntarism.

McCormack concludes his chapter on action-research with the reflection that 'context is a constant tussle between conflicting priorities where everyday practice is challenging, often stressful, sometimes chaotic and largely unpredictable' (2015: 310). Understanding context is a labour-intensive longitudinal process that unfolds to inform and respond to interventions over time. For the action-researcher, there is no convenient chronological start and end point. Somekh (2006) echoes this sentiment suggesting that action-research is cyclical and evolves until the point at which, 'a decision is taken to intervene in this process in order to publish its outcomes to date' (2006: 7). And, 'it is unlikely to stop when the research is written up'. Both these sentiments capture perfectly our interventions in Uganda. The publication of this book marks a stage in a journey and what we have learnt up to this point.

The remainder of the book guides the reader through our own learning processes as 'action-researchers' reflexively managing and evaluating the Sustainable Volunteering Project.

## THE STRUCTURE OF THE BOOK

Chapter 2 discusses the first part of our journey in operationalising the SVP. This contextual learning predated the SVP and framed our initial application for funding. Our experience of deploying long-term volunteers in the context of the Liverpool-Mulago-Partnership made us acutely aware of the damaging effects of labour substitution. Years of missionary or 'helper' style volunteering have shaped a culture within which the dominant expectation in Uganda was that volunteers were there to gap-fill and substitute for local staff, enabling them to take time off work. And many volunteers, influenced by similar discourses, are often quite (naively) happy to respond to these expectations. Clinical volunteers have a much more powerful ethical commitment to the prioritisation of immediate patient needs over systems' needs. The chapter title 'First do no Harm' is taken directly from the Hippocratic Oath – the ethical statement governing the conduct of the medical profession and prioritising patient needs.[20] Chapter. 2 reflects on the balancing and persuasive process that this has involved and how the SVP has developed and operationalised the 'co-presence' principle to guard against the systems damaging effects of labour substitution.

Chapter 3 takes a chronological step forward to the point at which the SVP was actively deploying professional volunteers into roles focused on training and capacity building based on the co-presence principle. Our experience of the project's progress began to raise concerns that the emphasis on and conceptualisation of 'training' imposed by most organisations funding volunteering (and embedded in indicators of success) fostered a kind of fetishism – with training. Our research suggested that, in practice, and in the context of Ugandan human resource management systems, training was failing in many respects to translate into active learning and was, in itself, generating worrying externality effects. Rather than generating empowerment and improving health worker behaviour, it was tending to compound the kinds of dependencies and corruptions identified by Moyo (2009). Chapter. 3 draws on research evidence to expose the unintended consequences of interventions focused on forms of continuing professional development (CPD) 'training'. It describes the SVP approach favouring on-the-job co-working and mentoring over formal off-site courses. This approach increases opportunities for genuine learning and confidence in deploying new knowledge. More importantly, this reduces the collateral damage caused by traditional CPD interventions. Notwithstanding these 'successes', our research suggests that the effects of even these interventions can be short-lived. It was at this stage in the project journey that we realised that co-presence, whilst essential, was not sufficient to guarantee knowledge translation and sustained impact. Ugandan public health systems are highly and actively resistant to change.

Chapter 4 marks the shift in conceptualisation emerging from both our own evaluation and learning but coinciding with wider policy agenda. The missing piece of the jigsaw it seems was the failure to understand both conceptually and in terms of operational dynamics, the step from training through learning to individual behaviour change. We have learnt that knowledge mobilisation does not automatically derive from learning; knowledge in itself is not empowering and may, indeed, be disempowering. Knowledge mobilisation is highly contextualised and needs to be understood within the frame of wider human resource management systems. In marked contrast to the approaches favoured in health sciences focusing on 'systematic reviews' of published research on similar (identical) interventions, we undertook a much broader horizon-scanning research review process. Our aim here was to identify any knowledge or ideas that could facilitate our understanding of the intervention–failure or systems stasis we were witnessing. Chapter. 4 reviews some of the work we identified and its impact on our learning and volunteer deployment model.

Chapter 5 applies the newly combined knowledge discussed in Chapter. 4 to two illustrative case studies. As we have noted, interventions in a project like the SVP take place and are modified over time. In many ways they represent a simple 'trial and error' approach underpinned by intensive grounded research to facilitate our understanding of change processes or change resistance. Tracking the identification of a 'need' and our experience of designing and monitoring the evaluation of that process, in the light of the new knowledge gained through ongoing research review improves our understanding of the complexity of social processes. Chapter. 5 redefines the objectives of our action-research project from the starting point where we believed we were setting out to capture the ingredients of positive change to one of pro-actively understanding and learning from failure. It attempts, in the context of this potentially debilitating reality, to take stock and identify the characteristics of least harm interventions to chart the next stage of our journey.

## NOTES

1. Annex 1 provides information on volunteer deployment in the SVP. In practice, SVP volunteers are drawn from a broad family of disciplines/cadres including clinicians, engineers and social scientists.
2. www.liverpoolmulagopartnership.org.

3. For details see www.liverpoolmulagopartnership.org.

4. This important dimension of the evaluation has been further supported by Health Education England funding. For further details, see http://www. salford.ac.uk/nmsw/research/research-projects/move. A companion book is due to be published (Ackers et al. 2016a).

5. The newly published Sustainable Development Goals (that replace the MDGs) cite a target MMR of below 70 per 100,000 births (UN 2015: 13).

6. These figures only capture recorded deaths in the facility and thus miss cases where mothers die in the community or where records are unavailable.

7. Staff–patient ratios differ enormously and more senior doctors are required to attend births on the private ward for which they are (relatively) generously remunerated. This does however suggest that training per se is not lacking.

8. http://www.mercyships.org.uk/mission-vision. We are aware that there is a great deal of controversy about the mechanics of providing emergency aid, especially in the post-crisis period.

9. UK and EU direct AID to Uganda was stopped in 2012 due to high-level corruption.

10. The term the *Daily Mail* used to describe it.

11. http://www.thet.org/our-work/what-we-do.

12. The Commonwealth Professional Fellowship Scheme is only one of many schemes offering fully funded fellowships to health workers.

13. Geographers increasingly use the concept of mobility to describe contemporary forms of highly skilled movement. THET defines a 'long-term volunteer' as someone who stays for at least 6 months. We would argue that stays of this duration would tend to fall within the frame of highly skilled migration (Ackers 2013, 2015; King 2002; Kesselring 2006).

14. Lord Crisp's report was written in response to an invitation from the prime minister and the Secretaries of State for Health and International Development to look at how UK experience and expertise in health could be used to best effect to help improve health in developing countries.

15. Full details are reported in Ackers (2013).

16. The numbers cited here are constantly increasing as we continue to deploy volunteers and assess impacts.

17. See Annex 1.

18. We have used the prefix UHW to identify Ugandan Health Worker respondents; FG for focus groups and V for SVP volunteers.

19. Two doctoral researchers, Hassan Osman and Natalie Tate, are currently developing dimensions of the research in Uganda.

20. This is also the subtitle of our sister book on Ethical Elective Placements (Ahmed et al. 2016a).

# 'First do no Harm': Deploying Professional Volunteers as Knowledge Intermediaries

**Abstract** Chapter 2 discusses the first part of our journey in operationalising the Sustainable Volunteering Project. It discusses the factors underlying the perceived 'human resource crisis' that is typically blamed for high levels of maternal and newborn mortality in low-resource settings. This is the environment within which professional volunteers find themselves and that they, and their deploying organisations, must negotiate with care. The chapter presents the risks associated with labour substitution or gap-filling roles and explains the importance of the co-presence principle to the SVP.

**Keywords** Human resource crisis · Labour substitution · Co-presence

## Introduction

Chapter 2 outlines the human resource context within which projects such as the SVP are deploying UK clinical volunteers. It begins with a brief presentation of global health 'metrics' emphasising the public view of the human resource crisis in LMICs. These stark metrics play an important (and intentional) role in stimulating the case for AID in all its forms including professional volunteering. Aggregate data on human resources in health form an important component of needs assessment. However, they are profoundly inaccurate in terms of conveying a statistical impression of health worker deployment on the ground due to the very poor and

© The Author(s) 2017                                                   21
H.L. Ackers, J. Ackers-Johnson, *Mobile Professional Voluntarism and International Development*, DOI 10.1057/978-1-137-55833-6_2

politically loaded nature of record-keeping. Furthermore, they present a profoundly distorted impression of the human resource context within which Health Partnerships and professional volunteers are attempting to promote capacity building. This chapter takes the reader through our own learning from the starting position where we assumed that we were engaging with the simple inability of LMICs to fund the training and deployment of health workers ('they need all the "help" they can get' approach) to our more contextualised understanding of the sheer complexity and power dynamics of human resource (mis)management. The immediate and obvious response to this simplistic 'health worker shortages' model is a labour substitution or service-delivery intervention. This response, whilst appealing to the altruistic and clinical learning needs of volunteers, lacks sustainability. It also undermines public health systems.

There is a strong tendency to assume that the solution to health systems crisis in countries like Uganda lies in clinical expertise and that clinicians are best poised to influence global health agenda. We have come to realise that this clinical expertise, whilst highly valuable, needs to be framed and managed within a much more multi-disciplinary and research-informed understanding of human resource systems. And this has important implications for the deployment and management of professional volunteers. The second part of the chapter introduces the concept of 'co-presence'. Co-presence is a well-known concept in the highly skilled migration and knowledge mobilisation literature and our familiarity with this framed our approach to volunteer deployment. Put simply, unless volunteers are working in co-present (or face-to-face) relationships with their peers, we run the risk of labour substitution and also fail to create the environment conducive to knowledge exchange and mutual learning.[1]

## GLOBAL METRICS AND FIRST IMPRESSIONS

The following section presents a brief overview of the some of the human resource problems that characterise Uganda's health system shaping volunteer engagement and goal achievement. According to the World Health Organisation (WHO), about 44.0 % of WHO Member States report to have less than 1 physician per 1000 population, and the distribution of physicians is highly uneven:

> Health workers are distributed unevenly across the globe. Countries with the lowest relative need have the highest numbers of health workers, while

those with the greatest burden of disease must make do with a much smaller health workforce. The African Region suffers more than 24 % of the global burden of disease but has access to only 3 % of health workers and less than 1 % of the world's financial resources.[2]

The clamour for metrics in the development/global health industry encourages the collection and aggregation of data which, perhaps unintentionally, drives policy agenda and intervention strategies. Table 2.1 summarises data from the WHO's 'World Health Statistics Report' (2010). It is important that we do not accept these figures as facts but approximations; numerous data bases report quite significant differences. However, the underlying message is clear: LMICs have far fewer skilled professionals than HRCs. In 2006, the WHO's World Health Report identifies a crucial threshold of 228 skilled health professionals per 100,000 population, below which countries were deemed to be in health workforce crisis (WHO 2006: 13).

Key stakeholders respond to this kind of data when designing their interventions. The Lancet Commission on Global Surgery 2030 (Meara et al. 2015) is just one example. Once again focused on 'global metrics', the Lancet Commission identifies five 'key messages', which include '5 billion people do not have access to safe, affordable surgical and anaesthetic care when needed' and '143 million additional surgical procedures are need in LMICs each year to save lives and prevent disability' (p. 569). On the basis

Table 2.1 Physician and nursing/midwifery density, regions and selected countries compared

| Location | Physicians | | Nursing and midwifery personnel | |
|---|---|---|---|---|
| | Number | Density (per 100,000 population) | Number | Density (per 100,000 population) |
| African region | 174 510 | 2 | 802 076 | 11 |
| **Uganda** | **3 361** | **1** | **37 625** | **13** |
| European region | 2 877 344 | 33 | 6 020 074 | 68 |
| United Kingdom | 126 126 | 21 | 37 200 | 6[a] |
| United States | 793 648 | 27 | 1 927 000 | 98 |

[a]This figure cannot be accurate. A recent UK report (HSCIC 2014) indicates that there are 347,944 qualified nurses in the UK NHS alone, suggesting a decimal place error
Source: World Health Organisation (2010: 122)

of this, they identify six 'core indicators', the second of which is focused on improving workforce density:

Kinfu et al. argue that the overall problem is 'so serious that in many instances there is simply not enough human capacity even to absorb, deploy and efficiently use the substantial funds that are considered necessary to improve health in these countries' (2009: 225). Although they don't single out development aid, this statement may well apply to this form of funding too. Their analysis suggests that current figures may represent a marked underestimation of staff shortages. However, data weaknesses preclude accurate analysis and even regional data 'mask diverse patterns' (p. 226).

The data presented above and typically cited focus on 'stocks' (overall numbers) but tell us little about how the existing workforce is deployed and managed on the ground and how foreign human resource investments (in the form of foreign expertise) can best be managed.

## THE HUMAN RESOURCE CRISIS IN UGANDA: CONTEXTUALISED KNOWLEDGE

The Ugandan Ministry of Health's Health Sector Strategic Plan III (MOH 2010) asserts that 'Uganda, like many developing countries, is experiencing a serious human resource crisis' (p. 20) restricting the country's ability to respond to its health needs.[3] It goes on to state that around 40 % of its human resource in health is working for the private sector (which includes the mission sector). One of the consequences of these shortages is a high proportion of unfilled vacancies in the public health sector. In 2008, only 51 % of approved positions were filled with vacancies reaching highest levels (67 %) in lower-level community-based facilities (p. 20). Facilities in urban areas and especially the capital city (Kampala) are less likely to experience problems with unfilled vacancies in comparison to more peripheral locations. The Strategic Plan reflects on the reasons behind this situation. And familiar concerns are raised over international migration ('brain drain') as health workers are attracted not only to resource-rich economies but also to neighbouring African countries such as Rwanda and Kenya where salaries are much higher and visas easier to obtain.

Other factors identified include insufficient training capacity, low levels of remuneration (forcing forms of 'internal brain drain' or deskilling as qualified workers move to other sectors) and poor working conditions.

However, even taking these factors into account does not explain the levels of staffing observed and experienced on the ground in Ugandan health facilities resulting in the pressures put on professional volunteers to gap-fill. The Strategic Plan goes on to identify low productivity as a result of 'high rates of absenteeism and rampant dualism' as the 'largest waste factor in the public health sector in the country' (p. 21). The World Health Report (WHO 2006) backs this up suggesting medical personnel absenteeism rates from 23 % to 40 % in Uganda (p. 190) and a World Bank Report (2009) quantifies the costs associated with absenteeism at UGX 26 billion. It goes on to identify the second most important source of waste as that arising from 'distortions from the management of development assistance', which constitute a 'major source of funding but are mainly off-budget' (World Bank 2009: 24).[4]

The ubiquitous 'human resource crisis' is repeatedly referred to in research papers in the field of 'human resources for health' (HRH) but remains underspecified with vague references to an overall lack of personnel and/or lack of necessary training and skills (Thorsen et al. 2012). Indeed, it is hard to find a paper that does not refer to the lack of skilled personnel in facilities as a major factor. However, the reader is often left wondering what lies behind this situation and what it means in practical terms for health workers and, in our case, professional volunteers. Generic reference to 'staff shortages' tells us very little about the situation on the ground.

When asked to explain the reasons for staff shortages in Ugandan health facilities, an experienced Ugandan health professional replied:

> To start with really they don't have enough people trained to fill all the possible positions. I know that almost all the big hospitals are advertising positions for doctors and nurses. I also know lots of doctors who don't want to practice as doctors because they can work as consultants in an NGO. They usually go to American funders, they basically look around everywhere for anyone interested in funding their opportunities. People are now trying to go for project jobs. One good thing that people have realised is you can work in a government institution because there you are guaranteed a lifetime job and, at the same time, there are so many projects that come into the government institutions and help people top up their salaries in one way or another (UHW).

The respondent identifies a number of contributory factors. In the first instance, he indicates problems in initial supply exacerbated by the haemorrhaging of doctors from clinical work into (usually non-clinical) positions in NGOs. Others strategically seek to combine 'project' work with their full-time public roles (contributing to absenteeism and exhaustion). The respondent later refers to the problems of international brain drain suggesting that many Ugandan doctors are looking for better-paid work across the border in Rwanda, for example. But this is compounded by the often more damaging but neglected effects of 'internal brain drain' (Ackers and Gill 2008). In Uganda, this manifests itself in many doctors studying for Masters Degrees in either Business Administration (MBA) or Public Health (MPH), positioning themselves to work in NGOs in managerial positions.[5]

Linked to the above, remuneration is a key factor affecting the presence of doctors in public health facilities. At the present time, private work ('moonlighting') is, in theory, illegal. In practice, it is endemic. To some extent, this represents a natural and entirely rational response to low pay. The following Ugandan health worker explains both the need for salary augmentation and the importance of holding a position in the public sector to facilitate private work:

> Most doctors working in the private sector are working for themselves simply because they need to make a bit of extra money and that way they can even negotiate to take some of the patients from the public hospital to their private hospitals (UHW)

In reality, it is not so much that the private work 'tops-up' or brings in a bit extra – the balance is rather the other way around with private earnings dwarfing public sector pay. One specialist heavily involved in very lucrative fertility treatment referred to his public role as his 'charity work'. In other cases, doctors, most of whom do not own their own premises, clamour around NGO projects involving infrastructural investments in the hopes that the more attractive and functional facilities will enable them to attract fee-paying patients.

In addition to the low level of pay, serious administrative problems in many districts means that healthcare staff are not paid at all for months:

> Right now they are not paying them enough and it doesn't come on time. I know people who don't get paid for six months and they expect them to

carry on smiling, offering the best services they can when their landlords are chucking them out because they don't have money to pay (UHW).

This respondent had personal experience having waited for over 6 months to be paid (in this case by a university). Remuneration remains a major problem but it is never the only factor (Garcia-Prado and Chawla 2006; Dielement et al. 2006; Mathauer and Imhoff 2006; Stringhini et al. 2009; Mangham and Hanson 2008; Mbindyo et al. 2009; Willis-Shattuck et al. 2008). And, it is not at all clear that a recent MOH initiative to significantly increase the pay of doctors in HCIVs (to 2.4 million per month – around £500) has translated into (any) increased presence on the ground.

In a rare study focused specifically on the absenteeism of health workers, Garcia-Prado and Chawla (2006: 92) cite WHO statistics indicating absenteeism rates of 35 % in Uganda. The reality is far worse. A senior manager of a Ugandan Health District reported (in an interview in 2015) much higher genuine rates of absenteeism, suggesting that during a personal visit that week, he found that over 65 % of his staff are 'on "offs"' at any point in time. This certainly confirms our experiences as ethnographic researchers and is likely to significantly over-estimate the presence of doctors. On one of the facilities we are currently involved with, the in-charge doctor has not been present at work for over 4 months (for no apparent reason).

Whilst overall health worker–patient ratios are relatively very low and many positions for which funding has been committed lie unfilled, it remains absolutely clear from our interviews and ethnographic work that the staff who are appointed and receive remuneration are very often not present for work. And the more senior the position the less likely they are to be present. In the following focus group with Ugandan midwives and doctors, respondents were asked about health worker absenteeism. They talked at length about midwives and nurses but did not mention doctors:

*Interviewer:*               You haven't mentioned doctors at all?
                             (Laughter between everyone)
*Respondent 1 (midwife):*    Oh, sometimes we forget about them because
                             most of the time we are on our own. You can
                             take a week without seeing a doctor so we end
                             up not counting them among our staff.
*Respondent 2 (doctor):*     Especially on a night, you never see them there (at
                             the health centre).

| | |
|---|---|
| *Respondent 1:* | Even during the day like most of the time. |
| *Interviewer:* | How often would you say a doctor would come to the facility in a typical month? |
| *Respondent 1:* | The medical officers have the rest of this centre to cover too so maternity will see them only if there is any problem. So they come for two hours three times a week but that's for the whole centre, the other wards as well. |
| *Respondent 2:* | Yes, like two times a week, sometimes once but most of that time even when they're on [duty] someone will not come to review the mothers. |
| *Interviewer:* | What would happen if a mother needs a caesarean? Would you call the doctor? |
| *Respondent 1:* | Initially they told us we should call before [refer-ring] but every time you call that doctor he is going to tell the same thing: 'I'm not around, you refer'. And you use your own judgement but sometimes you follow protocol, because if anything hap-pens... you call that doctor for the sake of calling. |
| *Interviewer:* | Just going through the process? |
| *Respondent 2:* | But you know he's not going to come (FG) |

In another location, the facility manager (a nurse) explains that, at the time of interview, there were few other factors restricting the use of the operating theatre (for caesarean sections):

*Now we have constant power – the power is there. We had issues of water now they've stabilised. Now water is flowing; the issue of drugs, we have sourced drugs.*

*Interviewer: But the doctors are still not here?*

*No, they don't even come and you have to keep calling. You will call the whole day and some will even leave their phone off. [Referring to a list of referrals] Take this [referral] is for a 'big baby' but this is a doctor, an obstetrician. [I asked] when you referred this case, why wouldn't you enter into theatre? We are making many referrals and the [hospital] is com-plaining. [The doctors] are very jumpy, they work here and there. So, we had a meeting and one doctor was very furious about [the decision to question referrals]. I said, no this is what is on the ground; we want people to work. And the reason [they give] is there's no resting room. There may be issues of transport (i.e. the doctors' personal transport), but there's also negligence (UHW).*

It is not simply that doctors work very few hours, but the unpredictability of their presence and the absolute resistance to commit to any set hours seriously impacts services and volunteer engagement. This situation has made it impossible for any of the facilities that we work in to run an electives caesarean section list, with the result that all cases become emergencies and are referred.[6] This not only causes serious delays for mothers but also makes it very difficult for professional volunteers to engage effectively with local staff and share skills for systems improvement.

Accommodation is a serious issue (as noted earlier), but it is not a panacea especially when it comes to doctors. In one case where our charity has funded a doctor's overnight room, it has yet to be utilised. On the other hand, where we have provided an overnight room for midwives (in another facility) we have achieved and sustained 24/7 working. Furthermore, in one of the health centres we are involved with where doctors benefit from the provision of dedicated (family) housing on site, this has not improved their presence. The following quote is taken from an SVP volunteer report:

> Caesarean section mothers operated on Thursday or Friday are generally not reviewed by a doctor over the weekend. One mother operated on for obstructed labour whose baby died during delivery had a serious wound infection, pyrexia and tachycardia and pleaded (4 days later) for me to help her (V).[7]

Another volunteer made the comments in a report she drafted for the District Health Officer just before she left:

> Medical attendance or lack of it caused many problems. [ ... ] in my own experience employed staff negate their responsibility when other professionals are on the ground believing that they will do their work and that they are free to work elsewhere (V).

She was referring here both to (foreign) volunteer presence but also to a visit by doctors from the National Referral Hospital during which time local doctors disappeared.

Whilst absenteeism and poor time-keeping are endemic problems amongst all cadres in Uganda, the situation is most acute when it comes to doctors. 'In-charge' doctors (senior medical officers appointed as facility managers) are often the worst offenders setting a very poor example to medical officers in their facilities and failing to observe and enforce contractual terms. As the following medical officer suggests, many if not most of the doctors in these leadership positions do not do any clinical work in the public facility they preside over:

> *Most of the (in-charge doctors), if you really look at them, want to do administrative work actually, they want to sit in the office – they sign out the PHC (primary health care) fund. It's at their discretion to spend it so.... And of course sometimes there's corruption, outright corruption.*
>
> *Interviewer: So really what they're doing is administration but not leadership.*
>
> *Leadership requires you to be around; you can't let people run the place when you're not there. Leadership needs your presence, so you know the fact that [the in-charge doctors] are not always there, it's difficult. (UHW)*

Where in-charges are nurses, midwives or administrators, they have very limited ability to hold doctors to rotas:

> [Enforcement] is a problem. Doctors don't want to be accountable to someone 'below' them. They don't want someone, even if someone has a degree but they're not a doctor, to keep instructing them. (UHW)

This problem of enforcement seems to stem from higher levels with District Health Officers (usually doctors themselves) seemingly powerless, or unwilling, to challenge poor behaviour:

> I think particularly in the health department they are still intimidated by doctors which is a bit surprising. It goes hand in hand with accountability because if I know I am accountable for something going missing and if it goes missing then something will be done to me; in terms of discipline then of course I will behave differently. I wouldn't want to be found doing something on the wrong side of the law because I know that there is action that is going to be taken against me. But because here people don't see anything being done then they can do lots of things. (UHW)

A recent audit conducted by a volunteer of referrals to the National Referral Hospital from a Health Centre IV facility clearly identifies the problem of physician presence. It is important to point out that there are five physicians employed to work in this facility – far more than most comparable health centres:

Figure 2.1 shows that 62 % of referrals relate to human resource issues with 59 % directly attributable to the failure of doctors employed in the facility to be present during their rota hours. The situation reported here is by no means unusual. In one of the Regional Referral Hospitals we are involved with the professional (obstetrician) volunteer has instituted a weekly maternal mortality review process. On average two women die every week in this facility. The weekly reports highlight the human resource factors contributing to deaths. In most cases, medical interns are having to take responsibility for the bulk of referred patients despite the fact that the hospital employs four consultants. These consultants are rarely present

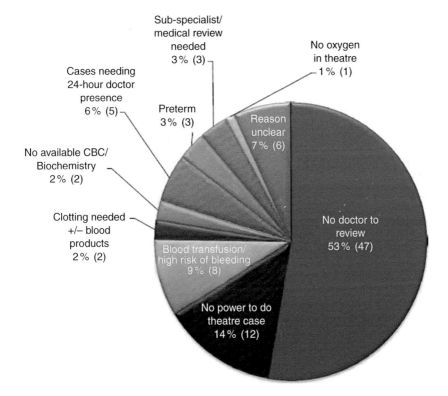

**Fig. 2.1** Primary reason for referral from a Health Centre IV to the National Referral Hospital (*Source*: Ackers et al. 2016b: 7. *CBC* Complete Blood Count. (Numbers in brackets are numbers of patients.) All rights reserved, used with permission.

when needed and health workers are anxious about contacting them to review patients. The following comment in the report is typical:

> Consultant was not called – intern was in theatre and gave verbal prescription. Intern and midwife felt unable to call consultant out of hours. Midwife perception 'not my place' and intern 'we are expected to cope with it'.

It is also interesting to note that since the review process commenced, none of the consultants has attended the maternal mortality review meetings. It goes without saying that this situation has a very serious impact on health systems, intern supervision and patient outcomes. Its impact on the effectiveness of professional volunteer deployment is less well recognised. On the one hand, in an environment where absenteeism is neither recognised nor punished, the presence of skilled volunteers actually facilitates it. It is more difficult from an ethical and visibility point of view for a Ugandan health worker to leave a ward with no staff (although this is common); the presence of a British health worker renders it much easier. In that important respect, labour substitution encourages both absenteeism and moonlighting. On the other hand, if a deploying organisation takes the (correct) view that permitting volunteers to work on their own in such high-risk situations is in breach of our duty of care, and fails to contribute to capacity-building objectives, then facilities in real need of additional human resource will be denied it. And, sadly this was the decision the SVP was forced to take in Wakiso District Uganda after over 3 years of engagement and unsuccessful dialogue with the District Health Office. In the absence of an understanding of the causes of low staffing, the very conspicuous absence of local staff effectively justifies and encourages gap-filling behaviour by volunteers.

The Independent Risk Assessment commissioned for the SVP added further impetus to these concerns. Identifying lone working or 'unsupervised clinical activity' as a key element of 'unacceptable residual risk' in some Ugandan facilities, the Risk Assessment took an unequivocal position requiring that volunteers 'withdraw from undertaking clinical work in the absence of professional Ugandan peers, or should they become a substitute for Ugandan staff – even if this leaves the patient at risk' (Moore and Surgenor 2012: 20). At the time we were surprised to find that the Risk Assessment identified Mulago National Referral Hospital as presenting the most serious risk of lone working (Table 2.2)[8]:

**Table 2.2** Residual risk exposure in SVP placement locations

*Summary Analysis*

| Hazard Profile | Over all Residual Risk Exposure (Taking Control Into Consideration) | | | | | | | | |
|---|---|---|---|---|---|---|---|---|---|
| | Kabubbu | Kassingati | Mulago | Kewempe | Mbale | Holma | Kisiizi | Mbarara | Gulu |
| Access to safe supply of food and drinking water at location | 10 | 10 | 10 | 10 | 10 | 10 | 10 | 10 | 10 |
| Assault (verbal, physical, sexual) | 10 | 10 | 10 | 10 | 10 | 10 | 10 | 10 | 10 |
| Unsafe or unsupervised clinical activities | 3 | 9 | | 3 | 3 | 3 | 3 | Unable to evaluate | 3 |
| Civil unrest/violent public disorder | 10 | 10 | 10 | 10 | 10 | 10 | 10 | 10 | 10 |
| Exposure to infection/tropical disease | 12 | 12 | 12 | 12 | 12 | 12 | 12 | 12 | 12 |
| Lone Working | 5 | 5 | | 5 | 5 | 5 | 5 | Unable to evaluate | 5 |
| Lost (in unfamiliar and/or dark surroundings) | 10 | 10 | 10 | 10 | 10 | 10 | 10 | 10 | 10 |
| Needle stick injury (including provision of emergency HIV post-exposure prophylaxis) | 10 | 10 | 10 | 10 | 10 | 10 | 10 | Unable to evaluate | 10 |
| Personal accident or injury including road traffic accident | 6 | 6 | 6 | 6 | 6 | 6 | 6 | 6 | 4 |
| Slips, trips or falls on uneven, wet and/or muddy ground | 6 | 6 | 6 | 6 | 6 | 6 | 6 | 6 | 4 |
| Sun exposure | 4 | 4 | 4 | 4 | 4 | 4 | 4 | 4 | 4 |
| Terrorist attack targeted at volunteers or projects (suicide bomb, false imprisonment, kidnap or hostage) | | | | | | | | | |
| Are all risk acceptable (i.e. controlled as low as reasonably practicable (Y/N)? | Y | Y | N Co-Presence & Lone working | Y | Y | Y | Y | N Unable to complete assessment | Y |

**Range of risk-exposure outcome scores (Severity x Likelihood)**

| Very low risk | | | Low risk | | | Medium risk | | High risk | | Significant risk | | | |
|---|---|---|---|---|---|---|---|---|---|---|---|---|---|
| 1 | 2 | 3 | 4 | 5 | 6 | 8 | 9 | 10 | 12 | 15 | 16 | 20 | 25 |

*Source:* Moore and Surgenor 2012: 20. (The Risk Assessment and a Policy Report based on it is available on our website http://www.knowledge4change.org.uk/. A version of this is published (Ackers et al. 2014).

This hospital in the centre of Kampala is, of course, the facility with the highest number of healthcare workers and one of the very few facilities in Uganda employing specialists.[9] The Department of Obstetrics and Gynaecology at Mulago Hospital (in 2014) employed 47 specialists, 48 senior house officers, 100 interns (17 at a time on rotations) and 350 midwives. These figures may seem reasonable in a facility delivering 30,000 deliveries a year. However, how can the risk of lone working be so high in such a context?

The reality is that staff are often not present on the ground during their contracted hours and it is very rare indeed to see any specialists present on wards; they are conspicuous by their absence.

A study by a local clinician on the 'Decision-Operation-Interval' examined the time that lapses between the decision to perform an emergency caesarean and the operation taking place and the causes and effects of those delays. Whilst lack of theatre space emerged as the dominant factor delaying operations, the report also identified a whole range of 'personnel factors' (shift change-over delays, absenteeism or late coming) underlying delays (Figure 2.2):

There is no scope in this book to discuss the consequences of low and unpredictable remuneration in any detail. Salaries are certainly below subsistence level requiring health workers to undertake additional work to make ends meet. The absenteeism that we witness is not a symptom of laziness or general demotivation; the more senior staff are typically very highly motivated and work very intensively deploying a high level of skill. But the overwhelming majority of this work takes place on a private basis. They are 'otherwise engaged' but often working long days and through the night with private patients and in private clinics or, in some cases, on NGO-funded projects. Shrum et al. had a similar experience in a project concerned with the installation of Internet communication systems in Ghana. Here, key players frequently failed to 'show up' for work. The authors make the subtle observation that, 'It's not that anyone was trying to do anything except their job.... It's that they have a lot of jobs' and were constantly engaged in trying to make money (2010: 160).

Absenteeism and moonlighting present specific challenges for programmes, such as the SVP, committed to avoiding labour substitution wherever possible. Put simply, where Ugandan staff are regularly absent and the risk of lone working is high, we are unable to place professional volunteers (Ackers et al. 2014).

| Rank | Factor | *Mean time lost (minutes), n = 351 | % Mothers affected |
|------|--------|-----------------------------------|--------------------|
| 1 | No theatre space | 366.5 | 94.0 |
| 2 | Shift change-over period | 26.1 | 22.2 |
| 3 | Instruments not ready | 15.1 | 21.4 |
| 4 | Surgeon on a break | 13.7 | 24.5 |
| 5 | Anaesthetist on a break | 11.7 | 6.8 |
| 6 | Theatre staff on a break | 6.4 | 13.7 |
| 7 | Some theatre staff not arrived | 5.1 | 12.5 |
| 8 | Linen not ready | 3.7 | 7.7 |
| 9 | Irregular patient drug dosing | 3.3 | 1.1 |
| 10 | Anaesthetist not arrived | 2.8 | 4.0 |
| 11 | No theatre sundries | 2.1 | 5.7 |
| 12 | Patient unstable | 1.7 | 2.3 |
| 13 | Patient not seen on ward | 1.6 | 0.6 |
| 14 | Lack of I.V. fluids | 0.5 | 2.0 |
| 15 | Patient not consented | 0.4 | 0.6 |
| 16 | Surgeon not arrived | 0.3 | 0.6 |

**Fig. 2.2** Common factors determining decision-operation intervals (*Assume all 351 participants.' doi: could be affected by all the factors. *Source*: Balikuddembe et al. 2009.)

## CHALLENGING TRADITIONAL VOLUNTEER ROLES: LABOUR SUBSTITUTION AND SYSTEMS DAMAGE

Whilst the concerns around risk in lone-working situations and the limited return on service delivery in terms of knowledge transfer and mutual learning are obvious, it is perhaps less immediately clear why substituting for local staff is actually counter-productive or damaging. Thinking in terms of the three hypotheses set out in Chapter 1, labour substitution may fall under Scenario 2: 'neutral impact'. And, certainly, if we believe the caricatures presented in the media and echoed in academic papers (that the human resource crisis in low-resource settings simply equates to poverty and pitiful staffing levels) then perhaps that is justifiable. Who could argue with the logic that overworked healthcare staff are exhausted and need a break?

The following section considers the role of professional volunteers from a more informed human resource perspective, arguing strongly that volunteer deployment must be framed and negotiated within an evidence-based understanding of local human resource dynamics. In so doing, it also emphasises the importance of multi-disciplinary expertise and not leaving these kinds of decisions to individual clinicians who may arrive in an LMIC with little understanding of human resource management in low-resource settings or even of international development.

The title of this chapter 'First do no Harm'[10] is taken from the Hippocratic Oath – an ethical statement governing the conduct of the medical profession. At face value, the Oath and its interpretation through the General Medical Council's 'Good Medical Practice' Guide (2015) do not suggest any major contradictions or tensions for doctors. Put simply, it requires doctors to pledge to put the needs of patients first and 'do no harm' to them. An earlier version of the GMC guide included a paragraph stating, 'Our first duty is to our patients, not to the Trust, the NHS or to Society' (2012). This implies a prioritisation of the one-to-one doctor–patient relationship – a highly individualistic approach to patient well-being which guards against political and pecuniary interference. However, it fails to grasp the potential unintended consequences of this approach when doctors are working as 'outsiders' in a foreign health system.[11] Hurwitz suggests that this simple message masks greater moral complexity in the face of 'bizarre moral predicaments' as 'new obligations thrust on doctors may conflict with their first responsibility to care for patients' (1997: 2). Although Hurwitz refers to the challenges of working in 'extreme circumstances', there is no explicit reference here to diverse international contexts. The updated (2015) version simply states: 'Make the care of your patients your first concern' (p. 0) potentially opening up opportunities for a more holistic interpretation.

The prioritisation of the doctor–patient relationship is often evident in the motivations expressed by professional volunteers applying for international placements through comments such as 'wanting to help people' or 'make a difference'. Many of the professional volunteers motivated to work in LMICs are motivated not only by clinical concerns but also by religious convictions. And these 'Good Samaritan' motivations often accentuate the desire to focus on individual patients rather than understanding and responding to systems.[12] Furthermore, whilst many professional volunteers – and especially those with prior experience in low-resource settings – articulate an interest in sustainability and longer-term change, they rarely interpret this as challenging their immediate commitment to individual patients. In other words, that systems change and immediate patient care may lie in some tension.

## Volunteer Roles and the 'Expectation of Labour Substitution'

Every time I turned up, everybody disappeared (V)[13]

This comment made by an SVP volunteer captures the experiences of the overwhelming majority of volunteers when they first arrive. Although we advise them to expect this prior to departure, it continues to shock. This experience is by no means limited to Uganda; indeed, it is a feature of most low-resource settings. Hudson and Inkson cite a respondent in their research on voluntarism who experienced this situation:

> A bad day is filled with frustrations and lack of understanding... all staff will have mysteriously disappeared (2006: 312).

Similarly, respondents in an evaluation of the International Health Links Scheme (Ackers and Porter 2011) expressed concerns about UK volunteers being left to work in the absence of supervision:

> We should say that we wouldn't send over junior British staff unless there's a senior [local clinician] on the wards and I wonder if that might set a bit of an example.

The SVP evaluation is peppered with similar experiences. In one example, a very experienced professional (short-term) volunteer described in his post-return report how, as soon as he arrived on the ward, the local consultant made an excuse that his partner was not feeling well and left – and then failed to return. The consultant in this case explained how, in the time frame of his short (10-day) stay, he managed to clear the backlog of untreated oncology patients and relieve congestion. Clearly, the patients were direct and immediate beneficiaries of this process but it would be impossible to justify this kind of voluntarism from the perspective of skills exchange or sustainability. And as soon as the volunteer returned to the UK, the wards would rapidly re-congest. Indeed, a more impactful response generating greater patient benefit in the long term may have been to reply 'I'm sorry but if you go I have no choice but to do the same'. This is the culture that we have been trying to embed within SVP relationships with an increasing emphasis on conditionality as relationships mature and mutual understanding grows.

In another quite different situation, the arrival of a group of American midwifery students at a Ugandan health centre was marked by staff absence. It is hard to say in this case if the arrival of foreign students encouraged staff to absent themselves – but they were certainly not planning to welcome them and the SVP obstetrician noted that the level of absenteeism was unusually high:

> The Americans have been covering up a shocking lack of staff at [facility] in the last two weeks which is good for the women but is making me grind my teeth. Essentially it seems that most of the staff have been individually summoned for trainings of various kinds by various agencies without any co-ordination with the sister or doctor in charge at the facility leaving us for days at a time without a neonatal nurse (V).

One of the most tangible signs of labour substitution is the placing of professional volunteers on staff rotas. And however much we discuss with the local partner, the problems with this is it remains a high expectation whether the visitors are consultants or students. We were aware of these tensions before the start of the SVP and issued clear guidance to all parties that professional volunteers should not be placed on staff rotas except in exceptional circumstances.[14] Quite understandably, local health workers are often upset about this and resent it, expecting volunteers to relieve them of very burdensome tasks. This reflects misunderstandings about the role of volunteers (and of Health Partnerships and AID more generally) accentuated by years of experience of missionary-style labour substitution voluntarism. Some local health workers will challenge the decision not to permit volunteers to go on rotas, suggesting that volunteers are work-shy voluntourists and more interested in going on safaris than supporting them. And this may well reflect their experience of volunteers. Challenging this culture of volunteering has proved a challenge within the SVP but we are confident that consistency in response is essential. The following Ugandan clinician who was part of a focus group argues forcefully against allowing volunteers to go on staff rotas on the basis that this will undermine co-working and encourage absenteeism:

> I don't support the idea that they go on the rota. I would not support that – they will leave all the work to her (the volunteer). I've seen it. Once you add

someone extra on the rota someone in that group will disappear for a year as long as they know the volunteer is there (FG).

Whilst this expectation was almost always experienced at the start of placements, it is by no means only at this stage. For most professional volunteers, it is an ongoing process involving complex negotiations at many levels. In one case, a volunteer who spent over a year in Uganda was constantly under pressure not only from her peers but also from the hospital superintendent (in this case, a British volunteer himself) to become involved in routine service delivery and be placed on local staff rotas.[15] She battled on a daily basis to resist service-delivery roles for over a year. Sadly, when she returned to Uganda after some months in the UK she immediately found that the expectation had increased. Staff assumed, as she knew the place and had experience of working there, she could immediately substitute for local health workers. In her monthly report she identified the '*main obstacles to achieving her objectives*' as follows:

> It's just that I seem to be left to do things on my own now a lot. Frequently I am doing the ward round alone with or without the intern as the only other midwife on the ward is in the Waiting Home for half the morning. Because I have been here so long the midwives treat me as one of the rota staff, which is lovely as they accept me and trust me, but means I can't do admin and prep for teaching as they assume I am always going to be there to do the ward round. And as there is often literally no-one else to do it I can't really just disappear to do teaching prep etc. so my objectives changed – I think that is probably a natural progression in this type of work after one has been there for a while (V).

This case has encouraged us to reflect on another deeply held assumption within the international volunteer deployment community and among hosts – that long stays are far more valuable in terms of development impact. The issue of length of stay is discussed in some detail in Ackers (2013). What is clear from the experience of this volunteer is that the presumption of gap-filling increased with length of stay and became very difficult (impossible) to negotiate as time went on:

> It would seem offensive now to the staff who I have got to know so well and so closely if I were to stop working the moment there was no-one to work with.

This situation may reflect a failure on the part of local staff to understand the role of professional volunteers, which may itself reflect a failure on the part of the deploying organisation, the host management team or the volunteer themselves to understand capacity-building approaches to international development. In many respects, we are dealing here with trying to effect in-depth ongoing culture change in an environment in which many of the actors involved either don't understand or don't subscribe to that (systems-focused) approach. One midwifery volunteer describes her experiences:

> On my first day all the midwives left to have their lunch. I was the only midwife on the ward of 27 labouring or newly delivered women. I think there will always be difference in opinion as to whether we are replacement labour or not (V).

This presents serious challenges when placing professional volunteers in the Ugandan healthcare system where the lack of senior staff or their failure to be present on the wards leaves more junior staff and students in situations where they have to work on their own and outwit the bounds of their competency. Lone working without supervision is normalised for Ugandan healthcare staff and it is unsurprising within this culture that volunteers are expected to do the same. One UK consultant clinician explained in her report how senior staff 'walked off the ward' the moment she arrived. These are common (normal) experiences in Uganda. The following excerpt from a blog written by an LMP obstetric volunteer working in a facility delivering 30,000 babies a year (over 80 a day) illustrates the problem in more detail:

> The 2 weeks leading up to Christmas were the most intense weeks that I've had at [the hospital]. All of the Senior House Officers [clinical trainees] were on exam leave and to make matters worse the interns [junior doctors] were on strike because they hadn't been paid. I was the only junior doctor on the rota to cover labour ward, theatre and admissions (there would normally be 3–4 SHO's and 4 interns)! Two seniors [specialists] were supposed to be covering labour ward during the exam period, however often only one would turn up and go to theatre leaving me alone. One day no specialists turned up at all, so I wasn't able to open theatre when there were 8 women waiting for caesareans. A woman presented with cord prolapse so I had to take her to theatre but she was the only caesarean that got done. To say I felt vulnerable would be an understatement, and in true [hospital] style everything you could imagine happened: eclampsia, twins, breech deliveries, abruptions, ruptured uteri. One particular incident happened when I was alone in admissions. A woman arrived in a semi-conscious state following an eclamptic seizure,

and was having an abruption (premature separation of the placenta leading to heavy vaginal bleeding). It was very hard to auscultate a fetal heart beat and I feared the baby was dead. After delivering the baby with a vacuum it needed urgent resuscitation. I attempted to resuscitate the baby but it was futile, I didn't have a towel to dry the baby and the resuscitation equipment was broken. A very frustrating and upsetting day (V).

This volunteer was deployed via the LMP in the year prior to the SVP and her experience had a profound impact on project design. During that time, a HUB partner working in Gulu Regional Referral Hospital recounted the experience of a volunteer midwife who,

*initially put herself on the staff rota. However, the local midwives stopped coming in because they thought, 'Oh she is there so that's OK'. So she took herself off the rota and started to come in at different times and did an assessment and made decisions about where her work was best needed. So she wasn't on the rota because, especially when it came to the evenings, she was invariably the only midwife there. I had a long chat with some other doctors and they said they'd seen the same thing. Two young [volunteer] doctors turned up and all the senior staff went on holiday the next day and that's unacceptable. It's very difficult to extract yourself from that situation.*

The case illustrates the relationship between lone-working and competency with early-career volunteers often under serious pressure to perform tasks that fall outside their experience and confidence.

This situation is by no means limited to obstetrics and gynaecology. This is just the department we are most familiar with. And as the SVP began to recruit and place anaesthetists we became acutely aware of similar problems. SVP anaesthetic volunteers were being repeatedly put under pressure to open theatres on their own due to a lack of local specialists. This came as something of a surprise as Mulago was one of only three hospitals in Uganda with specialist anaesthetists, most of whom have been trained with support from the Association of Anaesthetists of Great Britain and Ireland (AAGBI) and partner organisations in the USA and Canada. The reality is that there is no shortage of specialist anaesthetists in Mulago. However, they are rarely present to fulfil their local public duties or to work alongside professional volunteers. The initial advice from the AAGBI was that we should only place anaesthetic volunteers in Mulago, Mbarara or Mbale where UK-trained anaesthesiologist were in post. One consultant anaesthetist volunteer spent her first 2 weeks in Mulago and reported on her early experiences following initial meetings with local staff:

As far as my activity in Mulago [I plan to have] a non-clinical role as my working hours coincide with the presence of skilled and experienced anaesthetic staff.

Several weeks later, her perspective shifted when the reality of working in the National Referral Hospital became clear:

Staff absences and late starts are endemic and my presence alleviates the situation at times. As I have spent more time in Mulago I have got caught up in service provision. I'm feeling stressed, exhausted and like I'm failing on every front. The obstetric anaesthesia lead is rarely in labour theatre. There are always local practitioners (anaesthetic assistants) when I'm working but there has been 1 episode of me being the most senior anaesthetist on the floor with 3 Ugandan students for me to supervise. The senior Anaesthetic Officer (whom I contacted) who was supposed to be present felt no unease with the situation. The students' neonatal resus skills are not yet well established and I felt the whole setup left both me and the students exposed. The cases were of prolonged and obstructed labours and both mothers and babies were at high risk of complications.

There is a clear roster of who is on and the [Ugandan doctor] on a few occasions had tried to get hold of all of them who are absent. The surgeons are there. On the few occasions I was the first [anaesthetist] to turn up there and sometimes I have been there and there is nobody there. I don't know how people get away with it. Because if you look at the roster there are doctors during the day, nights and during weekends but there are no doctors [present].

As a result of this feedback and the volunteer being put in a situation where she had to open up theatre on her own, we requested that she work in other facilities. Similar experiences were had by anaesthetic volunteers placed in Mbale where the specialist worked almost all of his time in the private facility. Mbarara was a significant and unique exception. The consultant anaesthetist in Mbarara embraced the logic behind the co-presence principle before we even used the term issuing instructions to his staff that they must remain in the workplace until the UK volunteer herself left. This placement had proved one of the most successful with clear signs of sustained improvement many years after the volunteer left due in large part to the attitude of the local mentor.

The final case presented here took place during the professional Risk Assessment process and was picked up by the risk assessors in their report (Moore and Surgenor 2012: para36):

> 36. As a condition of ethical approval by the Hospital Ethics Committee, we were told that medical students were required to work during the weekends and at night. Both the volunteer and medical students spoke about difficulties accessing senior medical colleagues during the night. We were informed of a particular night shift wherein there were 2 still births, a death on the Maternity HDU and an obstructed labour – obstetric and midwifery staff apparently refused to attend and assist because they were sleeping (which we were told is normal practise and they are not to be disturbed whilst sleeping). We understand it was left to volunteers to work through the problems as best they could. Medical students explained how they were often goaded into carrying out clinical examination or diagnostic procedures they did not feel competent to perform, and whilst they declined to carry out the procedures, they explained how this created some tension with Ugandan medical students also working at the Hospital. We were concerned here about the level of clinical supervision and support, but also the security implications of working at night.

This case was also reported to us by the volunteer, resulting in a formal complaint and the promise, on the part of the Ugandan facility, to investigate further. We were not aware that this took place. In fact, the British obstetrician did wake one of the sleeping Ugandan doctors who then refused to assist her and complained at being woken up. The British doctor reported this situation in the patient's medical notes precipitating angry exchanges as Ugandan doctors pressurised her to remove the comments. This incident took place in the final 2 weeks of a 12-month placement causing serious anxiety for the volunteer. And, the pressure to undertake data collection during the night (on the part of the British medical students) came from their UK obstetrician supervisor keen to gain round-the-clock data collection for his research paper. When we contacted the obstetrician about this he responded defensively expressing the view that 'clinical' mentoring should and could be distinguished from risk assessment. In other words, risk was not his problem:

> Risk assessments are really issues for [sending organisations] rather than clinical mentors and I would not like to [get involved].

Sadly, service-delivery roles are also a direct response to the demands of foreign visitors, often keen to gain access to patients and conditions that they are unable to achieve at home. One of the worst examples of service delivery we have witnessed in Uganda – in this case entirely focused on training American doctors – is described by an SVP volunteer:

> *The Americans have kind of taken over (one of the obstetric) theatres. They have got some senior residents in special training and they have got these really junior doctors who are increasing their caesarean section skills. They have been here for a month just doing a lot of sections. They work during the day shift.*
>
> *Interviewer: So their objective is to train the US junior doctors and they take up the whole theatre? Are there any Ugandans in there then?*
>
> *No, I think they have been doing this for several years they have got introduced to everybody in one of the morning meetings and one of the guys said we have been coming here for six years.*
>
> *Interviewer: So, you think the main point is to train the American junior doctors because they cannot get that access over there (in the US)?*
>
> *Yeah (V)*

This situation is entirely unacceptable and unethical – even if it did mean that Ugandan mothers were being treated for free during that period with US equipment and staff. Not only does this type of intervention undermine the Ugandan health system, but it also caused problems for SVP volunteers attempting to achieve a level of co-working with local staff.[16] The following paediatrician contemplating applying to the SVP describes her experiences of volunteering as a medical student and her concerns that these forms of gap-filling voluntarism generate dependency:

> I'm not sure whether to go again. I first went to Uganda in 1985 as a medical student to a mission hospital. All the doctors and nurses there were ex patriates. They had their fingers in the dyke really. Although the medical superintendent was Ugandan and they did a great job looking after patients when they were there, there was no succession planning. There was complete dependency on the foreign staff. I guess it was a mission hospital model (V)

## CO-PRESENCE AND KNOWLEDGE BROKERAGE

The previous section has discussed the risks and unintended consequences of labour substitution models of volunteering. Chapter 1 described THET's mission in terms of 'leveraging the knowledge and expertise of

UK volunteers to build human resource capacity'. Clearly, deploying volunteers to replace local staff does not begin to operationalise that goal. The emphasis on knowledge in THET's mission could, arguably, be achieved through other forms of intervention such as donating books, providing on-line training or increasing training opportunities in the UK. It goes without saying that British health workers represent an important resource. They possess valuable knowledge gained through undergraduate education and subsequent continuing professional training and experiential learning. Of course, this is a diverse population and their skills, knowledge and personalities will vary widely. The fundamental question for projects such as the SVP is how can this resource (i.e. the embodied knowledge of UK health workers) be mobilised and deployed to offer optimal benefit to the Ugandan public health system? And what added value does flying them out to LMICs (human mobility) bring?

Our familiarity with the research on highly skilled migration and knowledge mobilisation made us aware of the complexity of knowledge itself and how difficult it is to simply 'move' it from one context to another and expect it to stimulate innovation or behaviour change. Although we are aware how complex these debates are, it is useful to summarise them here if only to help us understand what we mean by 'knowledge' in the Health Partnership context.[17]

Williams and Balaz (2008b) distinguish various types of knowledge suggesting that some forms of more explicit knowledge (such as technical skills) may be transferred internationally via text or virtual means. He contrasts this with 'embodied' knowledge where learning takes place through doing, is highly context-bound and requires greater co-presence (or face-to-face interaction[18]) and stronger relationships. Meusburger similarly identifies a 'missing distinction' in debates around the spatial mobility of knowledge, between knowledge and 'routine information' suggesting that, 'codified routine knowledge that can be stored in databases has to be distinguished from intuition, foresight and competence based on years of experience and learning' (2009: 30).

Whilst it is useful to identify explicit and tacit knowledge as opposite poles along a continuum, in practice, the categories are fluid (Meusburger 2009: 31). And the distinction begins to lose its significance when it comes to the *application* of knowledge. The capacity-building and systems change objectives of Health Partnerships demand highly complex forms of knowledge transfer, combining technical skills with mechanisms for their translation into socially relevant outcomes. In that sense, even much standardised forms of knowledge (clinical skills) need to be complemented with highly contextualised knowledge to support effective implementation. As Williams notes, while it is important to distinguish different types of knowledge, 'one of the keys to their valorisation is how they are combined' (2006: 592).

Williams and Balatz's paper on knowledge transfer in the case of returning Slovakian doctors opens with the assertion that, whilst health worker migration is an 'inescapable feature of the health sector... there has been relatively little research on mobility as a conduit for learning and knowledge transfer' (2008a: 1924). The paper identifies a range of knowledge acquired by doctors including 'technical skills, academic knowledge, cultural knowledge, management know-how and administrative skills' (p. 1925). They suggest that whilst some knowledge may be transferred electronically perhaps through reading and published protocols, other forms of 'embodied knowledge' are 'rooted in specific contexts, physical presence and sensory information and may include participation in clinical practice'. And these forms of knowledge are 'grounded in relationships between individuals' and in socialisation processes. The successful application of knowledge combinations, according to Williams and Balatz, requires 'co-presence' (2008a: 1925). The authors describe the opportunities for actors in this knowledge exchange process to act as 'boundary spanners' operating in places of 'unusual learning' where perspectives meet. And the conditions for this higher level of comprehensive knowledge exchange are not simply met by crossing national or other boundaries but by the quality of relationships at those boundaries (p. 1926). Meusburger contends that understanding the 'spatial mobility of knowledge' demands awareness of communication processes (2013: 29). Even where levels of explicit knowledge/skills are deemed higher in the UK, complex communication and strong relationships are required in order to contextualise that knowledge and translate it into effective practice in a Ugandan healthcare facility.

Meusburger is quite right to identify a range of 'assumptions' that shape the quality of relationships, including the impact of asymmetric power and the importance of non-verbal communication emphasising the importance of co-presence or 'F2F' contact. He also usefully distinguishes the types of individuals involved on the basis that knowledge may move differently between different kinds of stakeholders and practitioners and identifies a number of factors influencing relationships and communication process.

These include the 'cognitive abilities, ideology, interests, motivation, attention, emotions, and prejudices of the recipients and the milieu they are embedded in' (2013: 33). The emphasis on communication here is essential but in the context of multi-lateral exchanges. And participants in this co-learning process will bring different forms of knowledge to the table.

In order to achieve the goals identified earlier – with a strong focus on co-learning to support systems change – Health Partnerships need to focus on identifying mechanisms to facilitate the kinds of relationship-building conducive to behavioural change. Co-presence is a necessary pre-requisite for the kinds of relationship formation conducive to knowledge translation.

### *The Sustainable Volunteering Project and the 'Co-Presence' Principle*

Our experience of the risks associated with labour substitution or 'locum-volunteering' coupled with our research on knowledge mobilisation (albeit in a rather different context of scientific mobility) encouraged us to import 'co-presence' as a core operational principle shaping volunteer deployment in the SVP.[19] In this context, the doctor (or health worker) as a professional volunteer becomes a knowledge intermediary first and foremost rather than a 'carer'.

In practical terms, 'co-presence' simply means that UK professional volunteers should always be physically working alongside Ugandan peers in an environment that promotes opportunities for knowledge exchange. Co-presence does not imply that professional volunteers do not engage in clinical work. However, when they do so they must be appropriately mentored and engaged in active mentoring (according to their needs and the context). Co-presence is a composite concept representing the quality of relationships. Effective relationships play a number of distinct but related functions in the context of professional voluntarism. These include:

- The promotion of volunteer **safety** and mitigation of **risk** (discouraging lone working and ensuring compliance with competency principles).
- The facilitation of effective **knowledge transfer** (through training, mentoring and co-working).
- The process of embedding **reciprocity**, accountability and conditionality.

Implementing co-presence has been and continues to be a challenging process. It has met with resistance from not only local Ugandan staff (as noted earlier) but also some volunteers keen to optimise their opportunities for clinical exposure and often frustrated at the inability to intervene when local staff are absent. Nevertheless, we believe that is has begun to be understood and recognised as one of the features of the SVP. From an operational and evaluation perspective, it is implemented through a monthly reporting system which requires volunteers to state whether they have been able to comply with the principle and identify situations where the project managers need to intervene. This has been reinforced through regular interviews with volunteers and their hosts, site visits and bi-annual workshops. Co-presence now forms a core component of any Memoranda of Understanding governing relationships within the SVP and is increasingly subject to more concerted conditionality requirements. In more recent work it has shaped volunteer engagement in degree-level teaching and the functioning of the Ethical Electives Project (Ahmed et al. 2016b).

## Summary

Following the discussion of objectives in Chapter 1, this chapter has outlined the dynamics of the human resource environment within which capacity-building projects, such as the SVP, deploy professional volunteers. The SVP, in common with most volunteering schemes, has faced the multiple dilemmas of attempting to place professional volunteers in contexts, often at the requests of senior managers, only to find them left to work on their own in high-risk and challenging service-delivery roles. Not only will volunteers find that many of the staff employed to work in these facilities are not routinely there but their very presence, as volunteers, will encourage others to absent themselves. And volunteers themselves (particularly doctors) perhaps motivated by ethical principles to respond immediately and unquestioningly to patient needs or, more commonly, by their own desire for clinical immersion and the opportunities to practice on complex cases, often enjoy and seek out such high-risk 'Ninja'[20] medicine. Enforcement of co-presence is essential to change the culture of volunteering and the systems damage caused by passive and dependency-generating gap-filling. In that respect, co-presence must avoid becoming one of the conditionality principles that Moyo suggests have 'failed miserably' to constrain corruption and bad government because they were 'blatantly ignored and AID continued to flow' (2009: 39). Conceptualising professional volunteers as knowledge intermediaries in systems change interventions places a firm emphasis on the co-presence principle. Co-presence cannot guarantee effective learning, but it is a pre-condition of it.

## Notes

1. Co-presence is also central to risk mitigation in the SVP (Ackers et al. 2014).
2. http://www.who.int/gho/health_workforce/physicians_density_text/en/.
3. Some of the material presented in this section is published in Ackers et al. (2016b).
4. The 'off-budget' quality of this AID enables it to avoid accountability procedures, leaving it open to corruption.
5. In a rather different (post-earthquake) context, Dr Pokharel, vice-chairman of Nepal's National Planning Commission, responded to criticism of the Nepalese government's response by suggesting that the 'huge salaries on offer in NGOs and the UN are causing a brain drain in Nepal's civil service. 'A government guy gets $200 a month, whereas you are paying $2,000 per month at an NGO, which is damaging' (reported in Cox 2015).
6. We discuss elective sections in more detail in Chapter 5.
7. In a pilot project, our charity has recently constructed purpose-built accommodation for a Ugandan obstetrician in order to enable a regional referral hospital to attract a suitable candidate (they were faced with the prospect of having no obstetrician present at all which also meant we could not place long-term volunteers there). We have attempted to link conditionality principles to occupancy to ensure that the doctor works to his employment contract. We are currently monitoring the project. This work has been undertaken in conjunction with a sister charity 'One Brick at a Time' (OBAAT). For further details see www.lmpcharity.org.
8. The Risk Assessment and a Policy Report based on it is available on our website http://www.knowledge4change.org.uk/. A version of this is published (Ackers et al. 2014).
9. Few Regional Referral Hospitals have specialist obstetricians on their staff.
10. This is also the title of our sister volume on ethical elective placements (Ahmed et al. 2016b) and a short item in the RCOG International News 2015 (pp. 32–33).
11. Of course, there are issues here also around private medicine that fall outside the scope of this book.
12. Volunteer motivations are discussed in Chatwin et al. (2016).

13. Some of the material presented in this section is published in Ackers, Lewis and Ackers-Johnson (2013) in a paper on risk.
14. We permitted it for a short time when a student examination period coincided with an intern strike.
15. This was an unusual placement in a Mission Hospital which was part of the HUB.
16. This is one of many cases where foreign NGOs undermine each other and confuse local health managers.
17. For a discussion of knowledge mobility in the context of research, see Ackers (2013).
18. The term 'F2F' is used by some authors as an equivalent to 'co-presence' (Taylor et al. 2013). For more discussion of the operationalisation of the co-presence principle see Ackers and Ackers-Johnson (2013 SVP Policy Report 1).
19. For more details see the SVP Annual Report 2013 http://www.lmpcharity.org/images/documents/SVP%20Annual%20Report%202013.pdf.
20. A phrase used by a junior doctor to describe his volunteering experience.

# CHAPTER 3

# Fetishising and Commodifying 'Training'?

**Abstract** Chapter 3 examines the effectiveness of traditional capacity-building roles focused on the provision of training through Continuing Professional Development (CPD) or Continuing Medical Education. It draws on research evidence to expose the unintended consequences of interventions focused on forms of CPD 'training'. It describes the SVP approach favouring on-the-job co-working and mentoring over formal off-site courses. This approach increases opportunities for genuine learning and confidence in deploying new knowledge. More importantly, this reduces the collateral damage caused by traditional CPD interventions. Notwithstanding these 'successes', our research suggests that the effects of even these interventions can be short-lived. It was at this stage in the project journey that we realised that co-presence, whilst essential, was not sufficient to guarantee knowledge translation and sustained impact.

**Keywords** Continuing professional development · Continuing medical education · Conditionality

## INTRODUCTION

Chapter 1 set out the objectives of capacity-building approaches to international development as exemplified in the Tropical Health and Education Trust's Health Partnership Scheme and the focus this places on knowledge leverage to support systems change. In this context,

© The Author(s) 2017
H.L. Ackers, J. Ackers-Johnson, *Mobile Professional Voluntarism
and International Development*, DOI 10.1057/978-1-137-55833-6_3

we have conceptualised the role of the professional volunteer as a 'knowledge intermediary'. Chapter 2 emphasised the critical importance of context to the effective placement of such knowledge intermediaries and the damaging unintended consequences that may arise from labour substitution roles. This logically implies a highly specified, structured and supported role for professional volunteers focused on (bi- or multilateral) knowledge mobilisation. Indeed, the risks associated with labour substitution may be entirely mitigated by a role delineation explicitly prohibiting clinical work. And, many 'free mover' short-term volunteers (outwith organised programmes such as the SVP) have effectively chosen this option in order to avoid working without clinical registration[1] and professional indemnity insurance. In such cases, the desire to avoid complex legal and financial systems effectively drives the activity leading to a focus on fly-in-fly-out short courses.

Again, logically, these goals may imply a focus on initial (classroom) education taking place within the frame of education providers (colleges and universities). This would have the longer-term benefits of systematically training the next generation prior to their entry into the workforce. Deploying volunteers outside of health facilities, in formal (off-the-job) training encounters could protect them from the kinds of risks associated with clinical practice and increase their ability to focus on training. And, arguably, this approach, implying a focus on formal training, offers possibilities for substitution of physical presence with alternative (or complementary), environmentally responsible (low carbon) and cheaper modes of intervention. There are a number of reasons why professional volunteering, in the context of health partnerships, has tended not to focus primarily on initial education.

THET's Health Partnership Scheme (HPS) generally fosters or supports hospital–hospital relationships. In practice, this is less the case now than it used to be as universities and professional bodies (such as the Royal Colleges) are actively engaging in the HPS. Having said that, the pressures on organisations such as the Tropical Health and Education Trust to demonstrate value for money (and impact) have encouraged a focus on measurable short-term (in-out) interventions that are, at least in theory, amenable to metrics. THET fully acknowledges the importance of long-term relationships and the problems of achieving and capturing change in the short term. However, as with all funding bodies, project time frames are usually very short (20 months, for example) and THET are under pressure to demonstrate impact within these time frames.

Initial (diploma or degree-level education) is a longer-term investment and offers less potential for measuring specific and attributable systemic outcomes.

A second factor relates to the supply of professional volunteers. The majority of professional volunteers are motivated, at least in part, by their personal needs for learning and 'mobility /career capital'. International exposure has increasingly become a 'rite of passage' in medicine and other careers. Non-clinical placements are of little interest to many career track professional volunteers (Chatwin et al. 2016). As with funding bodies, professional volunteers are very keen to see change within the time frame and, wherever possible, directly attributable to their own activities. Whilst cautious progressive and collaborative incrementalism may be the most appropriate and effective mechanism for change in health systems, this approach may not appeal to funding bodies or volunteers.

Finally, and perhaps most importantly, it is widely accepted that education and training requires more than formal classroom teaching. Whilst classroom teaching may form a critical element of theoretical/ explicit knowledge acquisition, ensuring the learning of more tacit knowledge and implementation skills requires co-present learning 'on-the-job' through supervised placements and mentoring. The emphasis on 'lifelong' learning in the UK also places firm emphasis on structured continuing professional development to update and reinforce learning. This is the regime that professional volunteers and professional organisations (including the Royal Colleges) are accustomed to and therefore seek to replicate in Uganda. In other words, CPD is part of the culture of professionalism in the UK linked to professional development review (PDR). And, in that context, it does not translate, literally, into a more general interest in lifelong learning but implies short courses and an almost box-ticking exercise.

Chapter 3 responds to the following questions;

- What do you do with co-presence when you have achieved it?
- How do you deploy professional volunteers optimally as knowledge intermediaries?
- How do we encourage systems change relevant learning in this environment? Or, put more simply:
  - Who do we train?
  - What do we train?
  - How do we train?

## The Perceived Need for Continuing Professional Development in LMICs

There can be no doubt that there is a need for continuing professional development (CPD) or Continuing Medical Education (CME) in the Ugandan health system. This is not the same thing as saying that Uganda lacks the capacity to train its own health workers. The main need for CMEs and the one that is immediately observed by volunteers when they arrive is that the majority of staff they directly encounter on the wards dealing directly with patients and typically unsupervised are at junior level. Some hospitals depend almost entirely indeed on (unsupervised) student nurses and intern doctors to deliver services.

As we have noted in Chapter 2, this does not mean that there are no or even few very highly skilled and competent clinicians in Uganda but it is rare to find them on public wards or supervising/mentoring those staff who are. During a short (two week) visit, a senior British obstetrician working on one of the busy obstetric theatres in Mulago Hospital expressed dismay at his initial experience referring to the 'sheer butchery' he had witnessed. It was only later that he was made aware that all of the doctors in theatre were much junior interns with little experience or supervision. Add to this the overwhelming congestion and sense of chaos made worse by the absence of effective patient management systems (and triage) and it is not surprising that volunteers identify an immediate need for training. And perhaps this impression – of abject need – and absolute lack of resource – is functional in terms of attracting AID. On that basis, local managers may hesitate to challenge this naïve prognosis.

This situation has led to an emphasis in health partnership interventions on CPD or CME, a term used more commonly in Uganda and perhaps reflecting once again the dominance of the medical paradigm. Another factor reinforcing this emphasis on short-course interventions concerns the emphasis within internal (project) evaluation processes on easily obtainable metrics. The following caption frequently displayed by THET to promote the HP scheme indicates the emphasis on training and the challenges of trying to capture more holistic impacts on human resource management systems. The data presented here capture the easiest metrics: numbers of people trained. And measuring this is far easier if staff are taken off the wards and put into rooms where they can be counted. Unfortunately, this tells us nothing about the effectiveness of interventions and their impact on health systems (Fig. 3.1).

# THET AT A GLANCE

Over

## 41,200
global health
workers trained

## 26
Counties
in Africa
and Asia

## OVER

## 1700
NHS health workers have
volunteered with projects

Developing the
capacity of over

## 230
government & civil
society institutions

## 157
health partnerships
have received funding
and support

# ACROSS 14 HEALTH SPECIALTIES

- Maternal and Newborn Health
- Sexual and Reproductive Health
- Accident and Emergency
- HIV/ AIDS, TB & Malaria
- Child Health
- Eye Health
- Mental Health

- Non-Communicable Diseases (NCDs)
- Palliative Care
- Surgery
- Medical Engineering
- Occupational Therapy
- Blood supply
- General Health

**Fig. 3.1** Numbers of staff trained in the health partnership scheme (*Source:* THET 2015)

Having said that, we fully understand the challenges facing organisations like THET under pressure from their own paymasters (DFID) and seeking to justify the expenditure of public funds on development interventions in a time of austerity and swinging cuts in public services. Not only is this form of AID 'hard to get right', as Bolton (2007) suggests, but it is also incredibly difficult to capture. And providing the evidence base demands highly sophisticated and time-consuming approaches which fail to sit easily alongside the 'smash-and grab' demand for 'objective' (read quantitative) proxy outcome indicators.

The dominant approach to improving care [in low-income countries] (as a result) involves continuing professional development but (as Byrne-Davis et al. point out), 'little is known about their impact on practice' (2016: 59). One might argue that the best way to deal with this situation is not to deploy British professionals as volunteers but to improve local human resource management systems to require senior staff to be present and take on training roles, and for the health system itself to develop CME systems rather than relying on foreign interventions. In the capacity-building work we are currently engaged in, in the area of bio-medical engineering aimed at increasing the skills levels of practising technicians, we are beginning to lobby for the development of a CME system and to support the development of its constituent modules. At present, no such thing is in place.[2]

However, for the time being, this is the context within which professional volunteers will engage on a day-to-day basis. One might argue that training in itself is innocuous and can only add value. And, the more people we train presumably the more potential there is for positive systems change. One of the SVP volunteers expressed this view in an interview and in response to a question about the role that volunteers could play in system change:

> I don't even know how [a volunteer] would go about [engaging with systems]. There are so many levels of mistrust and corruption. Where to even start to infiltrate the system and go about it in the right way especially if you're a foreigner trying to come in and introduce policy. It's not even a can of worms. It's like a reservoir of snakes. Education is something you can't take away from someone and so that's something we can do continually, teach and set an example and then it's up to that individual if they carry on what you have imparted.

As the respondent notes – this approach is aimed primarily at individual clinicians and not systems as such. To the extent that a system is the sum of its constituent parts, then training individuals may in the very long term have a systems impact. Or, the individuals could become so demotivated (threatened even) when trying to utilise these skills on an individual basis that they either give up or leave the system.

Certainly it is essential that deploying organisations (including foreign NGOs) adopt some humility and accept outright that they cannot begin to train all the health workers in Uganda and, as such, this individual ('drop-in-the-ocean') approach is unlikely to generate systems impact.

## THE COMMODIFICATION OF TRAINING: SHORT COURSES AS PERSONAL INCOME

In high-income countries, training is unashamedly commodified: CMEs are a commodity that individuals (or their employers) often pay a very high price for. And, failure to engage in these forms of portfolio training linked directly to compulsory and structured professional development review (PDR) have an immediate and serious career impact. In that respect, treating training as a marketable commodity is not novel. The commodification process in LMICs rather turns this on its head. In this situation, health workers expect to be paid in order to train.

In practice, we have identified some serious unintended consequences associated with formal training. It has been traditional in Uganda and is now quite expected that CMEs delivered by foreign NGOs take place off-site in hotels or educational facilities. This has two immediate effects. First, it takes staff off clinical duties in an environment when wards are already barely staffed. And there is no culture or system for providing staff cover. It is not at all unusual when we find no staff present to be told that they are 'on a course' as if training can ever be a justification for leaving neonates unattended. Referring to a recent visit to a low-resource setting, a colleague at a meeting on global health in the UK reported:

> It was the most depressing visit I've undertaken – all key staff were away on courses elsewhere.

Secondly, people attending these CMEs generally expect to be paid a 'per diem' (daily top-up) plus expenses. In an environment where wages are so pitifully low, CMEs have become a precious and competitive commodity. It goes without saying that foreign NGOs are entirely responsible for this situation, creating, as Moyo predicts (2009), new opportunities for absenteeism and corruption.

## WHO ARE WE TRAINING: 'WE NEED SOME MOTIVATION'

This request, made to us repeatedly, was at first taken at face value to imply, literally, that staff felt deflated and low in spirits, given their levels of remuneration and working conditions. It soon became clear that the verb 'motivation' is being used rather differently, as a noun, to ask for money.

It is interesting that Mathauer and Imhoff explain how, in Benin, the term 'motivation allowances' is used to describe financial incentives to attend training and go on to explain how that has 'changed the meaning of motivation from a state of mind to that of an incentive [ ... ] giving the word a new meaning' (2006: 6). In effect, this has devalued training as an investment in its own right and created perverse incentives to lobby for and attend formal training.

A focus group involving three Ugandan health workers who have worked alongside many SVP volunteers expressed a similar experience when asked about the progress of SVP involvement in their facility:

> What I will talk about is the motivation because the times I have been with health workers going to workshops, it is a case in Uganda if they go for a workshop they think they will get a transport refund or per diem. I think that's what has made it not go on very well. Because they think your [SVP] volunteers come for training, you just train them but they will not get any per diem so they tend not to attend the workshop.[3] I think it doesn't work very well just because most people in the public sector think of money. The health workers in the public sector think of money. That's what I have seen. Sometimes the [SVP] volunteers would organise CMEs but most of the staff were talking about money. Are they going to give us some money? So most of them did not attend. Or if they happen to attend they come in for 30mins and see if they are signing [for expenses] and if there isn't [signing] they will walk away. Others come at the end of the session [just to sign and claim expenses] (FG).

His colleague then asks us:

> *How does that affect the volunteers and people like you? Because ultimately the volunteers want to train people so that they can work more effectively in adverse conditions. You know you [SVP] are doing a lot of jobs and you work long hours. How can you benefit the trainings the volunteers offer if people have such a mind-set? How will that shape the relationship with the volunteers and people like you?*

*[One of the participants responds] I think we should tell people we don't have any money to give. Yes, they should tell them that – there is always the expectation of money (FG)*

In another context, a workshop on placements involving a team of UK health trainers discussed frustrated attempts to achieve attendance at CMEs in Uganda and the constant pressure to pay per diems. One of the participants who had visited a Ugandan health facility on many occasions to do training stated:

We are told we have to take into account their passivity but it isn't that they are passive; it is that basically they don't want it (the training). Facilitation would help. If we put £62k behind it they would love the education but we are where we are. If we don't pay facilitation they won't come.

Other participants at this policy meeting agreed and suggested that paying per diems could be a solution to attendance problems. As participants in the meeting ourselves we urged them not to fall foul of the pressure to pay people for attending training. In the medium term this does nothing to encourage learning over and above ensuring that there are 'bums on seats' (trainees to be counted).

The distorting effects of per diems also have the effect of denying training to many clinically active health workers so that the same people – often those seeking to avoid clinical work – attend repeated training. Mathauer and Imhoff, again in the context of Benin, emphasise not only the wasted opportunity but also the tensions this can cause within staff teams:

Opportunities for training must be equitably allocated. They should not always privilege the same people (2006: 11).

The immediate association of CMEs and 'projects' with income colours relationships creating not only expectations of volunteers (in one case a UK doctor was referred to as 'Dr Donor') but also fomenting jealousies and suspicions. The following quotes from Ugandan health workers and cited in our Policy Report on 'Volunteer and Health Worker Relationships' (Ackers 2014) are typical:

When projects get involved everyone assumes that someone is getting paid (by the project) – that there are backhanders going on – so we need to be very accountable.

Interestingly the word 'project' in Uganda has its own quite specific meaning connected to large income streams and often US AID. 'Project' for many health workers simply means income stream.

> There is this mentality I'm sorry to say – that if you are associated with white people they think you are getting something in the office ... people need to be explained to, 'I am here to work. I am not paying people. I am here to exchange knowledge'.

Equity is an important issue and it is essential that clinically active front-line public health workers are immediately engaged in training. It is not always the case that senior managers (often doctors or clinical officers who refuse to engage in clinical duties in the public sector) attend the training. In some cases, SVP short courses have attracted staff cadres for whom the course has little direct relevance and where there is little, if any, chance that the skills will subsequently be utilised to improve patient services. Table 5 gives just a few examples of the cadres of students who presented themselves for a short course on emergency obstetric skills run by SVP volunteers. In this case, University staff organised attendance. One of the participants showing the greatest improvement in knowledge in post-training tests was actually a pharmacist. In the evaluation report, he noted that the 'main barrier' to using the obstetric skills was the fact that he was indeed a pharmacist.

**Table 3.1** Before and after test results on a CME on emergency obstetric care

|  | Before | After |
| --- | --- | --- |
| Nursing student | 7 | 16 |
| Midwife | 13 | 17 |
| Nursing officer/registered midwife | 14 | 16 |
| Nurse | 10 | 16 |
| SHO doctor | 14 | 18 |
| Ophthalmic nurse | 12 | 12 |
| Intern pharmacist | 5 | 14 |
| Public health student | 8 | 18 |
| Intern nurse | 15 | 17 |
| Nursing student | 6 | 13 |

*Source*: SVP data

In June 2015, the authors held a workshop in Fort Portal on human resource management in the public health sector inviting what we hoped would be the in-charges of all local facilities. At first we were a little surprised and even disappointed that very few of the in-charges came – even though the District Health Officer and the Secretary for Health in the Region were addressing the event. However, the final session, which focused on gauging the views of the audience, made us realise some of the reasons why the target audience (more senior people) had not attended and the real benefits of this in terms of providing a unique opportunity for clinically active health workers themselves to attend an event and express their views. It transpired that a conflicting event[4] was being held in the town sponsored by an American NGO which provided generous per diems. These opportunities were then immediately taken up by the senior staff leaving scope for others to attend our event which provided a meal and local transport costs only.

Asked in the final session to identify their main concerns in terms of HR management, delegates immediately spoke about what they called 'delegation'. At first we found this concept hard to understand until they explained that they meant delegation of opportunities to attend events and CMEs:

Delegation – somehow it is a problem in our health facilities – picking up knowledge is the most important thing about coming to these (training/knowledge exchange) days. [Managers] are not delegating to lower level staff – the in-charges are going on all the CMEs and they are not sharing the knowledge when they come back to the facility. So, for example, they may learn about hand washing but they are not sharing it so it is not becoming practice. The problem is the same people are going to all the seminars every week; others are not given opportunities: 'the work of my staff is to work and the work of the in-charge is to attend training'. The others are not getting access to the knowledge so it isn't affecting service delivery. Management can't delegate – this is the challenge (Participant 1)

My in-charge goes on one workshop then the next week he goes to another and another – there is no way of implementing the learning and no way that other colleagues can go. It is unfortunate the DHO [District Health Officer] has gone [left the meeting]. If the in-charge has attended a seminar 5 times then they should send other people – this is what Baylor [a US NGO] is now doing (Participant 2)

They attend too many workshops – the same workshop over and over again – they have not time to delegate or implement their learning (Participant 3)

One of the speakers suggested managers may need training in the art of delegation but it became clear that this was much an issue of personal income as lack of training:

> One of the problems is the implementing partners – the big NGOs organise many workshops and pay huge allowances so they all rush to those workshops and when there is a workshop where there is no money – everyone laughs – then, the point is – we get invited. If the in-charges get invited and there is no money they will delegate. Surprisingly the in-charges have communication with the organisers of the workshops and they know how much they will get paid- one million shillings etc. – so in fact we should make all workshops so people come here and pick knowledge without getting any money – they come away only with knowledge not money. If you got back with that knowledge and maybe a meal but no money you will go back with that knowledge and want to implement it.

One participant then suggested that, '*we should go back to all NGOs etc. and propose standardisation of per diems.*'

These comments emphasise the damaging effects that foreign engagement, even in such an apparently innocuous area as CMEs, can have and the importance of behaving responsibly and collectively. A study of the perceptions of per diems in the health sector in Malawi and Uganda (Vian et al.) came to remarkably similar conclusions that per diems resulted in unnecessary trainings, caused conflict, contributed to negative organisational cultures, fraud and 'were perceived to provide unfair financial advantages to already better-off and well-connected staff' (2013: 237).

Corruption is highly entrepreneurial and the incentives provided for training are a prime focus of such 'innovation' designed to extract personal gains from foreign partners and volunteers. A recent exchange involving a request for short course training for drivers of a motorcycle ambulance in Uganda is illustrative. In this case, we were requesting support from an HUB partner. The Ugandan lead willingly agreed to 'loan' us one their drivers trained by the Health Partnership for one week. When it came to payments we were taken aback by a request for us to 'provide his per diem of 150,000/ = per day for seven days'. This equates to a monthly salary of over 4,000,000 Ugandan shillings – ten times what a midwife gets paid. In this case we have learnt that such payments do not go to the individuals but involve a major top-slice (cut) for a number of intermediaries. Training becomes a lucrative gravy train and 'donors' are made to look like fools. This provides a very valuable example of how localised tacit knowledge trumps the apparent expert knowledge of outsiders; a point we return to in Chapter 5.

In conclusion, this section has shown how short courses have effectively become 'cash-cows' valued for the financial incentives typically associated with them. This has the damaging externality effect of restricting access to those health workers who most need training and reducing the prospect that training is used or shared. In response to our emerging understanding of this local context, the SVP has progressively moved away from any association with per diems and has actively campaigned to discourage the per diem culture. We have also encouraged the practice of holding CMEs as close as possible to the health workers' workplace to ensure contextual relevance and reduce the losses to clinical work. This has extended to active infrastructural work to provide high-quality training facilities proximate to hospitals and health centres.

The next section returns to a point made before, about the role of foreign intervention in CPD training. In the UK, CPD is viewed as a system with opportunities for review and progression and within the frame of workload management. It is not simply a case of doing random courses as and when they arise. This is not the case in Uganda. The view that all training is good coupled with the received wisdom that attendance at training (even if only to 'sign') provides a legitimate reason for absenting oneself from work coupled with personal financial gain results in a high demand for training. On arrival, a professional volunteer or organisation will immediately perceive this as a thirst for knowledge and respond accordingly.

Arguably, training needs to be valued as a commodity as it is in the UK, not to generate profits for training providers but to render training sustainable. The following quote from a leading member of the MOH in Uganda explains the dilemma:

[We have] reservations about funded programs because usually when the funding runs out, the life drains out too. Free trainings which are entirely dependent on funding are not self-sustaining, however, they can be sustained if the trainings are at a fee (minutes of meeting)

Notwithstanding the problems outlined earlier, CMEs undoubtedly constitute one of a range of potential knowledge transfer (often fairly unilateral) mechanisms. In that context, the next section considers the content of the training (curriculum issues).

## WHAT DO WE TRAIN (IN CMEs)?

When we first became involved in volunteer deployment in Uganda, one of the needs identified by UK doctors, perhaps fuelled by their initial exposure to clinical practice on the wards, was for 'emergency obstetric training.' And, the response was to develop short courses often based on established UK protocols with some adaptation to meet the rather different needs of a low-resource setting. At face value there can be no apparent problem with this. However, we became aware quite quickly of two concerns. First, that in an environment like the National Referral Hospital, any number of well-meaning NGOs from across the world could be devising such courses, based on their own national schemes and delivering them, often consecutively but on occasion simultaneously and often with the same cohort of staff (as noted earlier). A senior manager in Uganda made the following statement in a letter about CME input by international volunteers:

> We are happy to welcome colleagues from overseas but we need to ensure that their contribution is carefully evaluated, communicated and coordinated ... to streamline the system. This will add significant value to the sum of international development effort and enable us to build sustainable collaborations.

Present practices not only result in duplication but worse still, confusion, as the participants are unsure – when information conflicts – which approach to use. We also encountered a surprising degree of defensiveness and territorial behaviour on the part of foreign clinicians reluctant often to compromise on specifics when a more simple back-to-basics approach would have been far more useful in that context. And, secondly, following communication with the relevant Ugandan professional bodies, we found that there were national CME programmes in existence and being delivered in areas such as emergency obstetric care. The Ugandan Association of Obstetricians, for example, was actively using an adaptation of the Canadian ALARM course, as the basis for CMEs using obstetricians and midwives trained in the use of that programme. SVP volunteers suggested to us that these programmes were fit for purpose although senior clinicians working with international NGOs continue to argue over finer details restricting the potential for standardisation and local ownership.

Similar problems have emerged where foreign NGOs have intervened to teach neonatal resuscitation using their own protocols and found themselves overlapping with the Ugandan adopted 'Helping Babies Breathe' programme.

This duplication is certainly a major problem in contexts such as the National Referral Hospitals and other large facilities overwhelmed with NGOs. In other more remote areas, health workers may have received little attention from international NGOs. However, in practice, NGOs do venture to many places often 'imposing' (with the best intentions) their training schemes. Whilst communication with senior gatekeepers (such as the District Health Offices[5]) is often obligatory more active discussion with the relevant people on the ground and within the facilities is unusual.

It was interesting to meet two clinicians from a US NGO at a very small Health Centre III facility that we have been actively working in recently, setting up a training scheme for laboratory workers completely unaware that we had recently refurbished the laboratory and local staff were managing testing very effectively. One factor that tends to exacerbate this problem is the tendency of local managers not to advise NGOs about other actors on the scene in order to optimise engagement and opportunities for top-up payments and per diems. A British medical volunteer who contacted the SVP to discuss her potential involvement in training was clearly aware of this problem:

> I am very aware that when one visits these hospitals they are full of enthusiasm and make the visiting team feel not only welcome, but as if they are the only people helping. I have heard from other sources that both the Lifebox training and possibly the Safe Obstetrics course has already been delivered in [town], but apart from the WHO checklist in theatre, which is not used and a couple of lifebox oximeters, the staff deny all knowledge!!

An international conference on Healthcare Collaboration in Uganda held in Canada in 2014 (with very active Ugandan participation[6]) highlighted the need for improved communication and collaboration between external teams and with Ugandan leaders to encourage consistency in training; ensure awareness of the purpose of professional volunteers and promote mutual goal setting. A follow-up meeting between Professor Ackers and the Deputy Director of Mulago Hospital suggested that professional volunteers engaging in maternal health work were failing to work together, often generating confusion, restricting the effective transfer and application of knowledge and skills through unnecessary duplication and contradiction. Feedback from the SVP evaluation indicates parallel concerns among professional volunteers. In some cases, international relationships blossom into fruitful co-working. In others, volunteers are faced with unexpected and at times unwelcoming/competitive co-presence with other international volunteers.

## WHAT DO PEOPLE LEARN FROM SHORT COURSES?

We know relatively little about the impact that CMEs have on health systems in LMICs. This is not the same as saying people do not learn much but evidence that learning translates into changes in clinical practice, which in turn improve patient well-being and outcomes is elusive. One approach we have been encouraged to use in the SVP, more as the basis for external evaluation for THET, but also replicating approaches used in UK CMEs, is the practice of pre- and post-testing. These tests typically take the form of a simple multiple choice questionnaire focused on explicit clinical/technical skills. The tests are quite useful in capturing immediate (and explicitly clinical) knowledge acquisition and identifying areas where healthcare workers need further support.

## THE SVP EMERGENCY OBSTETRIC AND NEONATAL CARE (EmONC) TRAINING COURSE

SVP volunteers, in common with many others, were keen to engage in short course training in the area of EmONC. A short report (Tate 2014) describes our intervention in this area, which was integrated within an on-going mentoring and co-working programme. It was designed by an experienced British clinician who has worked for many years in Uganda and other African countries as part of the Liverpool School of Tropical Medicine 'Making it Happen' programme. In order to avoid taking staff off wards for too long, the SVP course took the form of an intense 2-day programme using

**Table 3.2**  Pre- and post-test results

| Role | Pre-course (%) | Post-course (%) |
|------|---------------|-----------------|
| Doctors | 77.5 | 87.5 |
| Registered midwives | 58.5 | 83.5 |
| Enrolled midwives | 62.5 | 81.5 |

*Source:* Tate (2014: 7)

mannequins in practical stations to encourage hands-on learning. We also used the conference room that we developed with a tent on hospital premises. The curriculum is focused on clinical skills including, for example, neonatal resuscitation, observation and early warning scores, management of eclampsia, sepsis and haemorrhage. A pre- and post-course questionnaire comprised 20 true/false questions including the following:

1. Low blood pressure is an early sign in haemorrhage T /F
2. Intravenous fluid should be given at a rate of 1 litre every 2 hours in hypovolemic shock T /F
3. Raised respiratory rate is a sensitive measure in shock T /F
4. In septic shock, patients should be given fluids at a rate of 1 litre over 20 minutes T /F

The tests results showed improvement in all of the participant's post-course knowledge (Table 3.2):

In this case, given the ongoing co-presence of volunteers on the wards, we were able to gain some feedback on the immediate impact of the training on staff. Volunteers noted improvements in their behaviour and practice:

> The midwives have shown improvement in their clinical practice and drug knowledge, as well as spotting and managing obstetric emergencies (V).

Working in Mulago Hospital with a junior doctor who had attended, a volunteer noted that observations were being taken with greater care and with closer attention to detail:

The interns were also sharing their improved knowledge with other interns on the ward, it was received with interest and enthusiasm and was actively being used in clinical practice. One recommended: The confidence with the improved knowledge was infectious (V).

A midwife participant also reported:

A few days after the course I had a patient overnight with severe PET, I felt I managed it better than I would have previously, I was confident to manage instead of referring (UHW).

On the basis of this experience we can assert, with some confidence, that the teaching is translating into relevant learning and that this is shaping individual practice and, on occasions, being shared with peers. The courses also provided opportunities to identify skills areas that prove a particular challenge to health workers. In one case, for example, an SVP neonatal nurse developed a CME programme involving short (2-hour) courses every week over a 6-week period (again delivered proximately on site). The test results showed overall improvement in knowledge with some significant weakness in their ability to understanding the mathematics behind dilution of medication for neonates. This enabled her to do further work on this area. It is difficult to say whether the staff later improved their practice mainly because the majority were not working on the neonatal unit and those who did were rotated out of it or left on a regular basis. Only one of those trained continued to work with our volunteer after the course ended. Staff rotation remains a persistent barrier to achieving any critical mass of trained staff in one facility/location capable of even beginning to change the culture and practice.

Another area which has a very high and continued demand for CMEs is neonatal resuscitation training in response to high levels of neonatal mortality and stillbirth. As managers of the SVP we are constantly asked to provide such training. However, the experience of professional volunteers working in the facilities indicates a very poor level of skills application. In one case quite shortly after the completion of this training, a baby was born in the facility requiring resuscitation; local staff were unwilling to use their skills and insisted that SVP volunteers resuscitated the baby. This may reflect a perfectly understandable lack of confidence in their new clinical skills – it is one thing to resuscitate a mannequin in a training room and quite another to resuscitate a newborn baby. But this experience

**Table 3.3** Improved outcomes as a result of short courses

| Indicator | Baseline | Endline |
|---|---|---|
| Partograph use | 4 % (Jan 2012) | 79 % (Feb. 2015) |
| Active management of third stage of labour | 5 % (Jan 2012) | 97 % (Feb 2015) |
| Screening for pregnancy-induced hypertension | 48 % (Nov 2013) | 68 % (Feb 2015) |
| Successful resuscitation of asphyxiated babies | 67 % (Aug 2013) | 81 % (Feb 2015) |
| Provision of essential newborn care services | 1 % (Jan 2012) | 85 % (Feb 2015) |
| Family planning counselling | 40 % (Jan 2012) | 91 % (March 2015) |
| Family planning update | 10 % (Jan 2012) | 67 % (March 2015) |

*Source*: http://savingmothersgivinglife.org/our-work/reports.aspx

is replicated across all facilities even where training has attempted to achieve a level of 'saturation', suggesting that training in many cases is failing to translate into behaviour change (implementation).

As we noted in Chapter 1, funding bodies and projects are understandably keen to 'prove their concept' and this results in the development of metrics that appear to suggest significant attributable outcomes. A recent blog by a senior Ugandan actor in an ambitious and highly lucrative USAID project (Saving Mothers Giving Life) is an extreme example of this. The short report claims overwhelming successes arising from what he refers to as 'high-impact interventions over a short period of time'. This statement is backed up by a table providing quantitative indicators of success (Table 3.3):

These figures purport to relate to public health facilities in the Fort Portal region – an area we are very familiar with. Sadly they bear little relation to the reality on the ground and create an entirely false impression that short course training immediately impact systems.

A far more cautious and in-depth review of another major training intervention funded this time by the UK's Department for International Development (DFID) of its 'Making it Happen' programme (Phase 2) presents data showing that between 2012 and 2015, 17,000 health workers were trained in emergency obstetric and neonatal care across 11 African countries.[7] The intense EmONC course is 6 days long and is delivered by multi-disciplinary teams using 'expert' volunteers. It aims to train a critical mass of 80 % of healthcare providers in the facilities involved. The programme has cost £18 million to date. However, the 2015 Annual Review refers to the 'difficulties of measuring the impact' and, on the basis of the data they could collect, reports that three out of the four outcomes are 'off track'. It is important to note that the report presents evidence of some post-course improvements but these are often quite minimal. Outcome 1, for example, aimed to increase the number of women attending participating healthcare centres for delivery by 20 % over 12 months: in practice, the improvement was around 1.5 %. And, Outcome Indicator 4: 'to reduce facility level newborn deaths by an average of 15 %' seemed to have failed with a reported increase of 44 % in just under half of the facilities. The point here is not to criticise this programme but to raise fundamental questions about the efficacy of short-term CME-style training and also the quite impossible metrics that funded projects are having to try to align themselves with. The Making it Happen report reflects on the need for 'qualitative research' to help provide a 'better understanding of the causes of deaths' and the impacts of the programme. It also suggests that more work needs to be done with governments to 'stabilise human resource situations' and 'reduce staff rotations', which undermine both the efficacy of training and the ability to control for and measure outcomes.

The effect of staff rotation ('turnover or transfer of trained health workers in the overseas institution') on the ability to embed and/or evaluate impacts is so well known that it is explicitly identified as a 'barrier to change' that applicants are required to respond to when making an application for THET funding (THET 2015: para 4.4).

In the SVP context, a strong pattern has emerged of rotation of Ugandan staff either during or immediately after training and mentoring interventions. In some cases, Ugandan healthcare workers have been transferred from the facilities or wards where volunteers have been work-ing as soon as training has taken place and in the absence of any commu-nication to either UK partners or the Ugandan health workers. Clearly, it is the prerogative of Ugandan authorities to manage their staff appropri-ately and this will imply moving staff at times. However, this practice has taken place following the return to Uganda of health workers supported for training in the UK under the British Commonwealth Professional Fellowship scheme and represents a significant loss of UK resource and disrespect for the scheme. In many cases, the re-deployment of Ugandan staff who have established strong relationships with volunteers and health partnerships appears to represent a deliberate attempt to break relation-ships and 'punish' Ugandan health workers. This may reflect a perception, once again built up through many years of voluntarism, that Health Partnerships are privately remunerating local health workers. This has a very damaging effect on health partnerships, on volunteer–health worker relationships and represents a highly inefficient way of deploying development resource.

Schaaf and Freedman document the effects of what they term 'Mission Inconsistent' (MI) posting in low-resource settings. They argue that the focus on 'calculating [skills] deficits and organising training' (2015: 1) has overlooked challenges that 'those who work on the ground' often see. And one of these is the effect of 'posting' or staff transfers on motivation. They identify two common scenarios. In the first place, health workers themselves may 'employ clientelism or bribery or obtain a post in a desirable area' (perhaps a location where they can optimise income from commodity sales or bribes). De Zwart (2000) refers to these as 'earning centres'. On the other hand, managers (as in the case earlier) may 'express displeasure' with a healthcare worker by re-locating them. This displeasure may be tripped by a perception that the health worker has established close (and potentially fruitful) relationships with volunteers or NGOs. Schaaf and Freedman conclude that in-depth qualitative methods are necessary to generate an 'emic understanding' of how posting and staff transfers are negotiated:

> Emic research will inform efforts that can work with the grain, by understanding the nuances of a particular social, political and economic context, and identifying avenues for meaningful change. (2013:7)

Consideration should be given to the idea of developing firm contracts with managers perhaps through Memoranda of Understanding (MOUs) or local 'Human Resource Compacts' with agreements to 'bond' or retain trained staff for periods of 3–5 years to enable the training to embed and project objectives to be achieved. Breach of these conditions should be responded to accordingly through a reporting mechanism to the Ministry of Health (via the Uganda-UK Health Workforce Alliance) and withdrawal of Health Partnership support. This is an area we are currently working to implement in the Fort Portal Health Partnership.

Intense off-the-job training via CMEs, in isolation, appears to be quite effective in terms of conveying explicit clinical or technical information in the short term at least. There is minimal evidence to show that this knowledge is retained or, of greater concern, utilised. And, our observational research within the frame of the SVP would suggest that there is little evidence that this is taking place. Of course, it is also difficult systematically to argue the opposite – that it is not taking place. What we are aware of is that when CMEs are embedded within on-going mentoring and reinforced through co-working during SVP volunteer stays the chances of knowledge translation and application are much greater. Some of the factors contributing to this process are as follows:

First, exposure to a new clinical skill may not lead to implementation because the knowledge is partial, not fully understood or because the participant needs supervision/support to enable them to use the skill for the first time. Confidence in actually using a skill is often built up over time in a supportive environment.

Secondly, from a knowledge perspective, the transmission of explicit clinical skills may not in itself be enough: explicit skills may need to be nurtured 'on-the-job' in combination with more highly contextualised tacit skills to begin to achieve implementation. And this tacit knowledge may be valuable both for the Ugandan health workers and the UK professional volunteers seeking to improve skills. Foreign fly-in-fly-out 'experts' are unlikely to possess the kinds of in-depth tacit knowledge that enables them to understand the healthcare context within which the 'new' skills could be utilised. Ironically, they are likely to be seen by many local actors as naïve and lacking in contextualised local knowledge.

## FROM TRAINING TO MENTORING
## (OR COMBINING TRAINING WITH MENTORING)

All you do is train, train train (UHW)

This comment was made to Professor Ackers during a review of the placement of SVP volunteers by a senior Ugandan midwife. She went on to urge the SVP to deploy volunteers in roles that 'enabled them to work alongside us – to work together'. Her point was well made and perfectly understandable in a small health centre IV facility that had so few local staff it could barely function and an in-charge doctor who refused to do any clinical work at all. In practice, the depletion of local midwifery staff exacerbated by the removal of doctors prior to completion of their fellowships in the UK (as a form of punishment) by the local District Health Officer eventually meant that co-presence was unworkable and we regretfully made the decision to withdraw.

Chapter 1 introduced the principle of co-presence as a necessary but not sufficient basis for effective knowledge exchange. Of course, co-presence is relatively easy to achieve in educational programmes and CMEs – to the extent that the co-presence is with students and learners. We would argue however that co-presence at this level requires also that professional volunteers are co-present with Ugandan trainers and educators – in a co-teaching format. This was the approach taken in the SVP EmONC course where Ugandan clinicians returning from advanced training at the Liverpool School of Tropical Medicine worked alongside their UK peers. Unfortunately, on the next planned delivery of the programme the Ugandan trainers demanded a much higher level of remuneration than previously paid (now that they had UK certificates!) and failed to join the training team. Their skills had become commodified and they were using them as an income-generation device, having set up their own training NGO rather than in their clinical work.

In a clinical context, co-presence is more difficult to achieve but absolutely essential to knowledge transfer and, more specifically, to the processes of knowledge translation and utilisation. Professional volunteers with clinical skills acquired from the UK need these relationships to be able to apply these skills in the very different cultural and resource context they find themselves in. And their Ugandan peers need this level of support and mentoring to build confidence to translate and apply skills learnt in CMEs. Building on our previous evaluation experience, the SVP began to focus on mentoring and co-working as the primary mechanism for knowledge translation and application.

## MENTORING, CO-WORKING AND KNOWLEDGE TRANSLATION

Our awareness of the limited impact and externality effects associated with formal 'off-the-job' CME training interventions combined with the risks and systems damage caused by labour substitution encouraged us to promote a mentoring approach to knowledge mobilisation. We have used the concept of mentoring rather than supervision to capture the bi-lateral co-learning and knowledge exchange quality of these processes. The idea has been to place professional volunteers, as knowledge intermediaries, into situations where they can work alongside their peers to promote learning-through-doing. This may both play a role in identifying the need for formal intense off-the-job training, perhaps creating opportunities for short-term 'fly in' clinical support or act as a critical follow on from this.

We noted earlier on the tendency for programme audit or internal evaluation requirements to skew interventions framed around the quest for metrics. Whilst we know that this approach to knowledge mobilisation is far more effective and less damaging than traditional approaches, it presents significant challenges in terms of project reporting (and perceived impact/success). Under pressure from THET to deliver regular quantitative data on training numbers, we invited one of the SVP volunteers to try to estimate her mentoring encounters. In the following excerpt, the volunteer (a British obstetrician) describes one working day and the kinds of mentoring she was engaged in:

> I teach all day every day and each session runs into others. If I give you an example of my day today you will see what I mean.
>
> In my ward round with 2 interns and a midwife the first patient was in obstructed labour at fully dilated. I discussed with them the use of syntocinon and how it should not be used in multips for augmentation. I discussed the indications and contraindications for instrumental delivery. I discussed with them the value of being able to ascertain positions and the likely causes of obstructed labour in a multip. The second patient was an IUFD at 35ks with a genital ulcer. We discussed the causes of genital ulcers, the investigations and treatments. We discussed the options for delivery including induction and the different methods of induction that can be employed. We talked about the riskes of doing an induction in a patient with a previous CS. 2nd patient cord proplapse with IUFD; we discussed management of cord prolapse and the best method of delivery in cord prolapse with IUFD.
>
> The third patient had premature rupture of membranes. We discussed the role of augmentation and antibiotics. The fourth patient had preeclampsia and was undergoing induction. We went through the signs and symptons of PET and the value of assessing them. We discussed the fact that syntocinon in the presence of intact membranes can cause amniotic fluid embolus. Would this count as teaching 2/3 people on 11 topics?
>
> I then assisted the intern at c-section. I talked him through what to do in a transverse section. He struggled to deliver the head so I took over. We then discussed techniques to help in the delivery of the head. I then assisted the intern at a second c-section. This one had a previous caesarean section and we discussed the likely complications and how to avoid them. We did the c-section and again I assisted with the delivery of the head. We talked

about the lack of tone and the deformities that made it difficult. I then went with an intern and a midwife to labour suite to see another woman with three previous c-sections and 4 normal vaginal deliveries and a malpresentation. We discussed risk of scar rupture and risk of cord prolapse. I did a caesarean section for a woman with 3 previous c-sections and a malposition. Prior to the c-section I took the intern through the delivery of breech at c-section (and at vaginal delivery). During the caesarean I discussed what I was doing and why. At all three caesarean sections I went through the theatre check list with the interns, including checking of the FH where appropriate. I also discussed with them both the importance of counting swabs afterwards and initiated this with each case. I did this in front of all the theatre staff and the anaesthetist, although not directly talking to them.

In the breaks between theatre I discussed a topic that we talked of yesterday, the exteriorisation of the uterus and closure of the peritoneum. I brought along some papers and evidence including Cochran reviews for this and we discussed it briefly. I encouraged them to go and read the papers then we would talk again.

At the end of the day one of the interns discussed with me the value of vaginal birth following caesarean section. We discussed this and the value of pelvimetry for about 30–40 minutes.

As individual teaching events to individuals this day I'm guessing in the hundreds. This is just one day, and it is not unusual. There is no way I could count individual teaching events in a month; it will be in the thousands. I could count hours involved in teaching, but it will probably be about 6–8 hours a day. I try to do no clinical activities without it being an educational exercise.

This discussion illustrates the complex and significant contribution the volunteer is making on a daily basis to knowledge mobilisation. However, it also shows how the pressure for evaluation metrics is tending to shape interventions and mentoring is a case in point. In many respects,

**Q – Our approach is to mentor health workers. How should we count the number of trainees?**
A - Please report to number of health workers you have mentored. You may need to ask your volunteers to tally them over the course of each reporting period.
**Q – We train health workers on the job. How should we count the number of trainees?**
A - Please report to number of health workers you have trained on-the-job. You may need to ask your volunteers to tally them over the course of each reporting period.
If you train the health workers in two distinct areas or topics, we would like you to count the health workers twice even though they are the same people. If you spread training on a single topic over a long period then please do not count the health workers twice.

**Fig. 3.2** THET frequently asked questions (*Source*: THET 2016)

it defies quantitative measurement. In recent months, THET has responded to this 'challenge' by producing guidelines on how to measure mentoring (Fig. 3.2):

We do not believe it is possible or methodologically appropriate to even attempt to capture data in this way. Certainly the results will massively increase the volume of 'encounters', but how should we interpret these? Fully capturing the effects over time and space of knowledge mobilisation through co-presence demands a quite different, more ethnographic, approach. Our experience with SVP volunteers suggests that mentoring is a far more successful mechanism for volunteers acting as knowledge intermediaries, providing a fruitful environment for mutual learning and doing. Having said that, we have to report the fact that in most cases the impact of even these interventions can be relatively short lived and rarely if ever extends beyond the period of co-presence. Where changes in behaviour are observed, there is typically a rapid time decay in implementation reverting to prior behaviour very quickly once co-presence ceases. One of the British Doctors involved in a Health Partnership described this experience as 'dipping your finger in a pool of water and then taking it out and watching the ripples disappear'. (Ackers 2014, Volunteer and Health Worker Relationships Policy Report, p. 2).

## CONCLUSIONS

Chapter 3 has built on the concerns expressed in Chapter 2 about labour substitution and its impact on Ugandan human resource systems. The chapter has exposed some of the problems and externality effects associated with the particular form of training that many, if not most, foreign organisations and professional volunteers are engaged in; namely, short courses or forms of continuing professional development. There is undoubtedly a need for continuing medical education as many of those health workers that volunteers directly encounter on the wards will be in need of additional training and support. However, the approach to CME provision by external bodies has developed into a culture in which training has been commodified – not to the extent that it is in the UK where the trainee has often to pay very high fees in order to receive training – but rather where the trainer is expected to pay learners for the privilege. In practice, this means that many of those people attending training are not intrinsically interested in the skills and many of those health workers who really need training are not given the opportunity to attend. Training also becomes one of a range of factors reducing (quite significantly in many cases) the amount of time more senior health workers spend in clinical work. Many doctors will never undertake clinical work in their public sector roles.

The kind of training that takes place off-site in CMEs may be effective in terms of transferring explicit technical or clinical skills but is unlikely in most cases to transmit the complex knowledge combinations essential to the effective translation and operationalisation of knowledge. When used in combination with mentoring and co-presence on the job, there is greater evidence of impact and skills utilisation and some real progress can be made. However, even in these cases, systems seem to be able to slip back as quickly as they progress once volunteer presence ceases. Why change is so short lived and so conditional on volunteer presence is a conundrum challenging many health partnerships. The 'exit strategies' that funding bodies and development organisations talk so much about appear hard to achieve in practice. Chapter 4 explores some of the reasons for the short-lived quality of systems change.

## NOTES

1. This is technically illegal but commonplace as many short-term volunteers operating outside the frame of structured (and funded) programmes are unwilling or do not understand these quite bureaucratic, time-consuming and expensive processes.
2. For details of the THET-funded bio-medical engineering project, see www. Salford and/or http://www.knowledge4change.org.uk/.
3. The SVP does not pay per diems as such but will cover essential expenses where necessary.
4. It is very hard to organise events without such conflicts arising as there is a received wisdom locally that it is best not to encourage NGOs to cooperate as this may reduce personal opportunities.
5. This is right and proper and the SVP has taken every step to build such relationships and ensure that senior managers are aware of and in support of interventions. It is however important to point out that in some cases local managers use this 'opportunity' to extract personal financial inducements; a kind of personal top-slice from all foreign NGOs as a price for permitting the engagement. This was another reason why the SVP, as a project, has withdrawn from engagement in Wakiso District.

6. Indeed, there were so many Ugandan obstetricians at this event which was followed by another event in Canada that some regional referral hospitals had to close obstetric theatres.
7. Annual Review 2015. The programme is implemented by the Centre for Maternal and Newborn Health at the Liverpool School of Tropical Medicine (CMNH-LSTM).

# Can (imported) Knowledge Change Systems? Understanding the Dynamics of Behaviour Change

**Abstract** Chapter 4 reviews a wide range of theoretical material in search of effective explanations for the intervention failures we have observed, and the resulting impact on the SVP volunteer deployment model. The step from training through learning to individual behaviour change was not fully understood conceptually or in terms of operational dynamics. We have learnt that knowledge mobilisation does not automatically derive from learning; knowledge in itself may be empowering or disempowering. Knowledge mobilisation is highly contextualised and needs to be understood within the frame of wider human resource management systems. Chapter 4 presents a critique of behavioural science theories, which have essentialising tendencies, and proposes ideas from evolutionary economics around 'imagined realities' and action planning which help to understand the contextual dynamics impacting on systems change.

**Keywords** Motivation · Behaviour change · Imagined realities · Action planning

## Introduction: Theoretical Insights from Diverse Disciplines

Chapter 2 discussed the importance of volunteer roles to an understanding of the outcomes associated with professional voluntarism focusing, in particular, on the risks and systems damage associated

© The Author(s) 2017                                                           79
H.L. Ackers, J. Ackers-Johnson, *Mobile Professional Voluntarism and International Development*, DOI 10.1057/978-1-137-55833-6_4

with service delivery and labour substitution. Drawing on theoretical insights and grounded research, the SVP operationalised the principle of 'co-presence' to protect against lone working and labour substitution and foster the kinds of relationships conducive to optimal knowledge exchange and co-learning.

Recognition of the externality effects (unintended consequences) associated with service delivery (by volunteers) has led to an increasing emphasis on 'capacity-building' amongst key stakeholders and funders. And, in most cases, this has been interpreted to imply that professional volunteers should be primarily engaged in training/education and knowledge transfer activities. Chapter 3 reported evidence of the role that professional volunteers (in carefully structured programmes) can play as 'boundary spanners' and knowledge brokers. However, whilst transferring knowledge is evidently possible, it also reflected on the failure of these approaches to stimulate and sustain lasting and effective systems change. Put simply, the knowledge is being shared but the impact is minimal and short-lived, rarely extending beyond volunteer stays.

Chapter 4 addresses the 'why' question: why is systems change so elusive even in an environment of carefully managed knowledge transfer, translation and exchange? These concerns, drawing directly on a wealth of lived/empirical evidence, stimulated the authors to search for theoretical insights capable of throwing light on the dynamics involved and informing future interventions. It is highly unusual to place a chapter of this nature towards the end of a book. The fact that it is where it is reflects the essentially iterative quality of our research journey and the inter-weaving of theory with empirical work. In this case, it is the empirical work that led to our search for new theoretical ideas to help us to understand our findings as they emerged and then, in turn, stimulate new empirical questions.

Theories exist to facilitate understanding and explain social phenomenon. Sadly, they are (almost always) associated with the construction of concepts and language that render them inaccessible to anyone outside the narrow disciplinary confines responsible for their development. Disciplinary silos tend to generate exclusive language that restricts the very objectives of theorisation (understanding) to the point at which small groups of people are essentially communicating only with each other. This chapter seeks to interpret a complex (if not comprehensive) range of theory to assess the potential for more holistic, multi-disciplinary, insights into the dynamics of health worker behaviour.

## Our 'Journey' through the Disciplines

As noted before, and discussed in more detail in Chapter 2, the whole process and more specifically, the SVP project, was profoundly shaped by theoretical work coming primarily from geography but drawing on other disciplines (business and education). Theories of knowledge and the conditions shaping its mobility across international space informed the development of the volunteer agreements, associated partnership agreements (Memoranda of Understanding with Ugandan partners) and, most notably in operational terms, the co-presence principle that lies at the heart of the SVP. As our evaluation of the SVP led us to question the efficacy and sustainability of interventions involving professional volunteers in terms of longer-lasting systems change and patient outcomes, we began to search for other ways of understanding these complex change/ inertia dynamics.

In the first instance, perhaps because our search was (somewhat unwittingly) influenced by the clinical focus of our Ugandan work (i.e. on improving maternal and newborn *health*) it took us directly to a burgeoning literature associated with the disciplines of behavioural psychology, implementation science and evidence-based medicine. We refer loosely to this collection of theories as 'behavioural science' (BehSci). In some respects, these theories share common ground with classical economic theory centred on the concept of the individual decision maker underpinned by ostensibly quantitative 'data'.

This corpus of work offered immediate and poignant insights into the relationship between knowledge/learning and individual behaviour change. And the work had a major influence on our thinking, encouraging us to conceptualise the 'problem' as one relating to behaviour change. However, as we explored the work in greater depth we began to realise that the concepts used, the approaches to the theorisation of knowledge and the associated privileging of quasi-scientific methods coupled with a profound emphasis on the individual failed to resonate comfortably with our research experiences and observations in Uganda. The BehSci literature examined the relationship between individual 'capabilities' and motivation. Ackers' background in socio-legal research and the supra-national impacts associated with European law reminded us of very different conceptualisations of 'capabilities' and encouraged us to revisit socio-legal theory, which itself draws heavily on social philosophy. This work takes us beyond individuals and organisations to more structural and over-arching elements of context and, specifically, the role that legal systems and social policy (sometimes referred to as 'soft law') play in shaping individual and organisational behaviour. Of particular interest here is the emphasis on agency and empowerment – on individuals as active citizens in complex and 'tiered' or 'nested' relationships with the State rather than as isolated and passive victims. This literature, which is primarily theoretical, also draws interesting parallels with philosophical concepts of positive freedoms (enabling social rights) sometimes known as the 'freedom to' (do something) as opposed to the more familiar 'freedom from' (laws protecting citizens from legally sanctioned behaviour). We shall refer to this very loosely as the 'capabilities approach' (CA).

The emphasis on employment in Barbard's socio-legal paper (2001) sparked an interest in another flourishing area of research focused on human resource dynamics. There is a considerable literature applying human resource management (HRM) ideas and theories to an understanding of health worker motivation in high- and low-resource settings. Interestingly, this literature focuses primarily on the organisational context and tends to be characterised by more qualitative (case study) approaches. Our first reaction to this body of work was to identify with the emphasis on organisational dynamics and the deeply contextual quality of these – something that is present but remains largely peripheral in the behavioural science work. And also to nudge us into a significant if obvious realisation that health worker motivation is fundamentally not a clinical question – so there is little surprise that 'evidence-based *medicine*' (with its origins in clinical trials) fails to capture adequately the dynamics involved and perhaps lacks the tools to do so.

Somewhat by coincidence (serendipity[1]) we stumbled upon another approach espoused by evolutionary economists but using language and ideas that, to us at least, seemed remarkably different to classical economics. This fundamentally theoretical work uses rather different concepts to discuss essentially the same challenge: how to mobilise knowledge in order to optimise outcomes.

We shall group the work reviewed here loosely under the heading of 'Evolutionary Economics' (EE). It will perhaps come as no surprise that this group of theories utilising concepts including 'imagined realities' and 'innovative intentionality' (as with the socio-legal ideas mentioned earlier) are unapologetically theoretical and largely untested in empirical contexts. It is perhaps for this reason that they are able to engage so luxuriously with context and imagination.

This chapter reviews the work referred to earlier. The aim here is to draw on our existing grounded empirical knowledge and experience to identify approaches and concepts that appear to be most relevant and offer greatest potential to an understanding of the role of the individual health worker in the advancement of health systems change in the Ugandan public sector. We have tried, wherever possible, in order to optimise engagement and inter-disciplinary communication to avoid excessive use of complex terminology and referencing. And we apologise in advance if this has failed or results in an over-simplification.

## INSIGHTS FROM THE BEHAVIOURAL SCIENCES (BEHSCI)

The Behavioural Science work reviewed here shares three key premises. First, that 'improving the implementation of evidence-based practice and public health depends on behaviour change' (Michie et al. 2011: 1). This focuses attention on the importance of individual behaviour change. BehSci theorists contend that, 'Progress in tackling today's major health and healthcare problems requires changes in the behaviour [ ... ] of healthcare professionals' (Michie et al. 2009: 1). Second, and this is where the attraction of the theory first sparked our interest, it explicitly recognises that knowledge in itself cannot change behaviour:

> For most health behaviours [ ... ] **knowledge is not an important source of variance** (Cane et al. 2012: 15).

This implies that knowledge in itself will not automatically generate capacity-building or systems change. To understand variance we need to look elsewhere. Finally, 'behaviour change techniques' form part of what proponents describe as the 'science and technology of behaviour change' (Michie et al. 2011: 2). This underlines the epistemological[2] underpinnings of BehSci theories; the privileging of 'scientific' methods and the inference (by reference to 'techniques') that change lies at individual level and that interventions targeted at that level can work.

The behavioural science literature reviewed here is applied to two rather different phenomena: first (and perhaps this is where the more clinical orientation derives from), it is used in public health contexts to try to improve patient behaviour (smoking cessation, addiction or healthy eating, for example). The same ideas are then applied to a rather different context; namely, the behaviour of healthcare professionals.

And, in this sphere, they are applied to more readily 'measurable' specific clinical behaviours (such as antibiotic prescribing).

Evidence that such interventions have largely failed to generate the intended impact have raised concerns that impact is limited not because of the quality of the knowledge transferred per se (or knowledge transfer mechanisms) but because the 'behaviour change intervention' is neither evidence-based nor theoretically informed (i.e. linked to a comprehensive model of behaviour). Michie et al. argue that interventions need to be designed so as to 'bring healthcare professionals into line with evidence-based practice' (2009: 1). A systematic review of published interventions by Michie et al. leads them to conclude that researchers were 'less confident about being able to replicate behavioural interventions compared with pharmacological interventions' (2009: 2). Attributing this to low levels of investment in research in this area (in comparison with pharmacology) rather than any more fundamental differences involved in comparing the relationships that humans have with inanimate objects (such as a statin or aspirin) with those more inter-subjective relationships that humans have with each other, they propose the development of a science or 'technology' of behaviour change to support accurate replication.

Whilst we would absolutely support their argument in favour of strengthening the reporting of observational studies, we would challenge the appropriateness of extending existing guidelines for the reporting of pharmacological research to analyses of health worker behaviour given the complex inter-subjectivity that the latter involves. Perhaps it is the language used and its reference to 'ingredients' and the 'science of behaviour' that makes us cautious about the applicability of these ideas to Uganda health workers:

> Just as medicines are described in detail in the British National Formulary (BNF) we need a parsimonious list (nomenclature) of conceptually distinct and defined techniques, with labels that can be reliably used in reporting interventions across discipline and country (2009: 4).

Working with another group of authors, Michie proposed the now familiar model of the 'Behaviour Change Wheel' as a 'method for characterising and designing behaviour change interventions' (2011: 1). The 'COM-B'[3] model is designed in the first instance to predict patients' responses to public health interventions around smoking cessation and obesity in England. It defines behaviour change interventions as those 'designed to change specified behaviour patterns' signalling a focus on individuals (as patients and healthcare workers). It is perhaps interesting to note that the emphasis at this point is not on understanding behaviour but changing it. Subsequent reference to 'behaviour change techniques' reinforce this assumption: dysfunctional individuals lie at the heart of the problem. Michie et al. outline the methods used to develop their model grounded in 'systematic review'. The concept of systematic review is very much linked to the evidence-based medicine movement and derives from methods developed through the Cochrane Collaboration.[4] The NHS Centre for Reviews and Dissemination (CRD) defines a systematic review as, 'a review of the evidence on a clearly formulated question that uses systematic and explicit methods to identify, select and critically appraise relevant primary research, and to extract and analyse data from the studies that are included in the review' (CRD 2001: 3)

There is no scope here to discuss and critique the relative merits of systematic reviews and their claims to objectivity. Certainly their value and approach in understanding clinical drugs trials is undisputed. For us, as social scientists more accustomed to the concept of 'literature' or 'research review', they present a certain narrowness in focus that may risk excluding highly relevant and innovative multi-disciplinary knowledge and/or grey literature (Benzies et al. 2006). The emphasis in systematic review processes on the 'clearly formulated question' tends to lead to a funnelling approach, progressively narrowing inquiry to an ever-smaller group of highly similar studies. Whilst this approach may form a key component of the comparability criteria necessary in clinically oriented systematic reviews (to compare like with like and reduce extraneous 'noise'), it lies in some tension with more expansive and exploratory 'searchlight' or horizon-scanning approaches to literature review explicitly seeking new knowledge and innovative insights (as represented in this chapter).

Furthermore, the 'quality appraisal' component of systematic reviews is based on the premise that research can be ranked according to its quality, reliability and replicability. In practice, this involves a weighting process based on metrics to assess 'the rigor of the research methodology' (Jones et al. 2013: 3) effectively privileging quasi-experimental techniques. At the apex of this epistemological hierarchy (Levels 1 and 2) lies the randomised controlled trial (developed from clinical research) and, at the base, opinion pieces. Qualitative research receives no specific mention in this schema but presumably falls within the generic category (Level 3) of 'non-randomised, controlled or cohort studies, case series, case controlled studies or cross-sectional studies' (Benzies et al. 2006).[5] We are also concerned that the notion of 'validated' tools appears to ignore the fact that the validation process may take place in a quite distinct context (UK- or US-based addiction studies, for example) and is then applied to a quite different context (health worker behaviour in low-resource settings).

Just as the systematic review process employed in this material has the tendency to encourage blinkered approaches and restrict the exploration of new knowledge, their approach to theory has the same effect. Cane et al. contend that, 'behaviour change interventions informed by theory are more effective than those that are not' (2012: 1). Certainly, a robust theoretically informed approach promises greater chance of success than what are often ad hoc, uncoordinated and often conflicting interventions. And 'opinion pieces' would generally not be published in peer-reviewed journals in the social sciences.

However, the 'comprehensive theoretical model' presented by Cane et al. involved engaging with 18 psychological theorists and 30 health psychologists (2012: 2). They were in effect talking to each other. The important point here is that concerns (that we share) about the lack of theoretical foundations are interpreted within such myopic disciplinary lenses. Interestingly, the authors propose that their integrative 'Theoretical Domains Framework' (TDF) developed through work with the aforementioned groups will 'make theory more accessible to, and usable by, other disciplines' (2012: 2).[6] This approach has parallels with surrogacy: the genetic map is intact and 'given' and the surrogate discipline is then able to apply it but not to re-combine it with its own knowledge to alter the essential architecture.

Having discussed some of the concerns underpinning the generation of behaviour change models, we now turn to assess the potential value of the models themselves in terms of supporting our understanding of the failure of professional voluntarism to stimulate sustainable health sector reform in Uganda.

The 'Behaviour Change Wheel' is described by Michie et al. as a 'potentially elegant way of representing the necessary conditions for a volitional behaviour to occur' (2011: 4). In this 'behaviour system', capability, opportunity and motivation interact to generate behaviour, which, in turn, influences these core components. Or, put more simply, individual behaviour change is the sum of an individual's

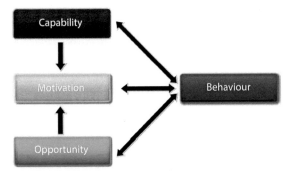

**Fig. 4.1**  The COM-B system (*Source*: Michie et al. 2011.) All rights reserved, used with permission.

capability (their knowledge and skills); the opportunities they have to utilise those skills and, critically, their motivation to do so. Much CME interventions, as discussed in the previous chapter, focus attention only on improving individual capability. These relationships are illustrated in (Fig. 4.1).

Whilst Michie et al. argue that this system gives no priority to individuals, groups or environmental perspectives – or intra-psychic or external factors – in controlling behaviour the emphasis in practice is very much on the individual. Capability in this model has a specific, individualised, definition – namely, 'the individual's psychological and physical capacity to engage in the behaviour' including knowledge and skills (2011: 4). Motivation is also defined in individual terms as 'all those brain processes that energise and direct behaviour' (2011: 4).[7] Finally, opportunity is 'all those factors that lie outside the individual that make behaviour possible or prompt it'. Michie et al. argue that this framework 'incorporates context very naturally [through] the "opportunity component"' (2011: 8). It is clear then that both capability and motivation are internal to the individual in this model.

The simple elegance of this model is what attracted us to it in the first instance. It immediately captures the errors behind the 'training fetishism' described in Chapter 3 and helps to explain why endlessly training Ugandan health workers in neonatal resuscitation or triage fails to translate into sustained behaviour change and improved patient outcomes. The concept of motivation has an immediate resonance too with ethnographic observations and the narratives of volunteer interviews. Certainly, at face value, the majority of employees in the public healthcare system in Uganda give the appearance of and readily describe themselves as 'demotivated'. And, it is all too obvious that the lack of opportunities to utilise skills due to lack of equipment, drugs or stationary inevitably leads to both a lack of motivation to learn and also a frustrating inability to exercise newfound skills. The logic of this model 'explains' why the deployment of professional volunteers solely to teach and train (transmit knowledge) is failing to impact systems.

The COM-B system outlined earlier is positioned at the heart of a 'wheel' which identifies potential 'intervention functions' and policy categories that may or may not form part of an intervention depending on the analysis of the situation and where the problem lies (Fig. 4.2).

In a further development, Cane et al. map their 'theoretical domains framework' onto Michie's wheel suggesting that the two approaches work together well in informing interventions (Cane et al. 2012: 12) (Table 4.1).

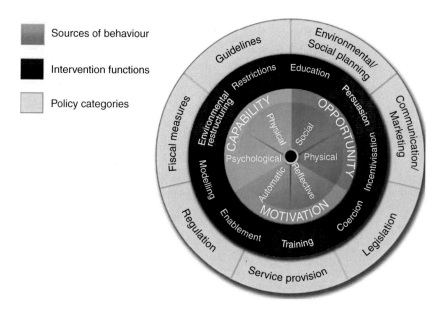

**Fig. 4.2**   The Behaviour Change Wheel (*Source*: Michie et al. 2011: 1.) All rights reserved, used with permission.

**Table 4.1** Mapping of the Behaviour Change Wheel's COM-B system to the TDF domains

| COM-B | | TDF domain |
|---|---|---|
| Capability | Psychological | Knowledge |
| | | Skills |
| | | Memory, attention and decision processes |
| | | Behavioural regulation |
| | Physical | Skills |
| Opportunity | Social | Social influences |
| | Physical | Environmental context and resources |
| Motivation | Reflective | Social/professional role & Identity |
| | | Beliefs about capabilities |
| | | Optimism |
| | | Beliefs about consequences |
| | | Intensions |
| | | Goals |
| | Automatic | Social/professional role & identity |
| | | Optimism |
| | | Reinforcement |
| | | Emotion |

Once the convenience of the model had sunk in and we began to consider more carefully how this related to our own experience and knowledge of volunteer engagement in Uganda, concerns emerged about its ability to capture the complexity of the real-world context. The explicit individualism of this model and the assumption that health systems are a collection of individuals rather than complex social and relational structures raised some concerns. In many ways, this is reminiscent of Margaret Thatcher's famous declaration that, 'There is no such thing as society. There are individual men and women and there are families' (**Interview in Women's Own 1987**).[8] The implied emphasis here is on dysfunctional individuals and the 'techniques' that can be devised to render them functional. We became particularly interested in the concept of 'capabilities' used here as something internal and reducible to an individual: a 'given'.

Certainly our understanding of health workers had made us very aware that the same person could show a high level of motivation and capability in different contexts. We have been involved in hosting many Ugandan health workers in the UK through the Commonwealth Professional Fellowship Scheme and with few exceptions in this context there is no evidence that they lack skills or motivation. Equally, staff members working on a private ward in a public hospital or in private clinics appear to work far more effectively than they do on the public wards. Does this suggest that capability is not an individual trait as such but contextual and also that 'opportunity' is everything?

## PERSPECTIVES FROM SOCIO-LEGAL STUDIES AND SOCIAL PHILOSOPHY (CA)

It was at this point that we reviewed some of the work on capabilities from the perspective of socio-legal studies, which itself draws on social philosophy and citizenship studies. This research would most certainly not be picked up in a systematic review. We have called this group of theories the 'capability approach' (CA). Once again, this literature uses complex concepts and language, potentially limiting accessibility and opportunities for holistic multi-disciplinary thinking. Barbard's paper addresses 'capabilities' from the perspective of the development of the European Union and its associated legal institutions. It is concerned primarily with the conditions necessary for the realisation of the European Council's strategic goal of becoming 'the most competitive and dynamic knowledge-based economy in the world capable of sustainable economic growth with more and better jobs and greater social cohesion' (2001: 464).

At first sight we may dismiss this work as somewhat peripheral to our concerns (with professional voluntarism and health systems in low-resource settings). The language used is more up-beat; less about 'problems' and more about knowledge for foresight and innovation. However, the immediate link with 'investing in people and combating social exclusion' lies at its heart. What initially interested us was the quite different approach to the concept of capabilities. Here they are not reduced to intrinsic or raw attributes of individuals but linked to concepts of agency and 'proactive security' (2001: 467). Barbard first critiques neoclassical economic theories which conceptualise what they call 'individual self-sufficiency' as a function of individual endowments, 'consisting of genetically-inherited capacities for work, and the financial and other resources made available to them' (2001: 465). In this model then outcomes are a function of inputs (individual innate ability) and resources. Drawing on the work of Sen (1999), Barbard proposes the addition of other functions identifying capability as 'a kind of freedom: the substantive freedom to achieve alternative functioning combinations' (citing Sen 1999: 75):

> Mobilising the economic potential of individuals is not simply a process of providing them with the necessary financial resources to exploit their endowments. Rather, the institutional framework of the market has to be examined in order to establish how far it facilitates or constrains the potential of individuals to achieve their desired economic functionings (p. 466).

Put simply, mobilising the economic potential of individuals is not simply a combination of innate endowments (intelligence) and resources (intellectual and physical). Capabilities in this approach are less reductionist and more composite than in BehSci theories: capabilities are not knowledge as such but mobilise (convert) knowledge. The practical example Barbard gives to illustrate her point helps to clarify the argument. Whilst sex discrimination law in the EU formally sanctions overt discrimination against female employees (a negative freedom or freedom 'from' discrimination), it is the more positive form of 'freedom to' sometimes referred to as soft law or policy, in the form of subsidised childcare or paid maternity leave, for example, that alters incentive structures enabling women to make personal investments in skills and training. Achieving gender equality demands both approaches.

For Barbard, individual behaviour (if we can phrase it that way) requires an assessment of how far the labour market (or the 'environment' in the COM-B model) facilitates or constrains the potential of individuals to utilise their knowledge and abilities. Barbard uses the concept of 'institutionalised capabilities' to describe the infrastructure of social entitlements (social rights and associated support) that facilitate and enable active participation. For Barbard, this infrastructure is not a luxury but a fundamental precondition of a functioning labour market providing the necessary incentive structures (proactive security) to enable and facilitate individual behaviour change. Indeed, the logic of this model is that, in the absence of institutionalised capabilities, investment in training is ineffective and wasteful: training inputs focused on generating changes in aggregate individual behaviour will not work. As critics of market liberalism have argued, society is more than a sum of its parts. And people need rights and resources to engage with knowledge.

Can this model be applied to the very different context of low-resource settings and the specific institutional context of health systems? We cannot see why not. Barbard's conclusion that the European Social Model needs to combine social rights, economic commitment with high-quality employment opportunities and industrial relations (dispensing with the idea that economic growth or institutional change can be achieved with a poorly skilled, low productivity, workforce) seems just as relevant to the Ugandan health system. And her proposal that such change requires a 'multi-level regulation' apposite.

Pfister (2012) similarly approaches capabilities from the perspective of European citizenship. Pfister suggests that Sen's 'capabilities approach', or 'CA', places important emphasis on individual freedom. He suggests that this can be further developed to situate individual freedom within strong relational and political elements:

> [The capabilities approach] is a powerful tool to put individual circumstances in the broader political, economic and social context (2012: 241).

Pfister emphasises the importance of context and differentiated needs to an understanding of the relationship between resources and functionings (or 'opportunities' and 'behaviour' in the COM-B model):

> Differences between persons with equal resources in achieving functionings should not be explained with purely individual intermitting variables, such as (lack of) ambition, responsibility or (wrong) personal choice. [Rather we should be attentive to] differences in the capabilities of people to turn resources into functionings (2012: 242).

Capabilities then are not a given; they are a product of the interaction of resources (opportunities) with agency. The CA perspective shares Barbard's emphasis on the role of the State (or of citizenship) in providing citizens with the 'positive ability' and encouragement to participate in society (or their own workplace) and invest in their own social capital and training. The concept of 'agency freedom' (the freedom to achieve whatever the person, as a responsible agent, decides he or she should achieve) is then introduced and linked to the notion of 'goals':

> We not only have to be able to achieve a goal but should be genuinely free to decide whether we actually want to achieve it or find an alternative

objective (even one which others might view as less beneficial to our well-being) (Pfister 2012: 243).

Pfister suggests that the CA approach does not go far enough in terms of shifting the emphasis from the 'individual' (*Homo economicus*) to the person as 'situated self' and the fundamental importance of context to an understanding of human interaction and relationships. He suggests that the CA approach underplays the importance of power relations and the 'positional' quality of relationships and 'struggles'. Pfister's comment that 'even entitlements to certain capabilities have to include a notion of who is responsible for providing them' (2012: 249) immediately resonates with our empirical work in Uganda, placing an emphasis not only on the individual health worker but also on their employing organisation or the State (Ministry of Health) to ensure that salaries are paid with some predictability (which they are not) and equipment and consumables provided. In this context, should the failure to remunerate be conceptualised as a simple lack of 'opportunity' as in the COM-B model or as a denial of fundamental rights (and disempowerment)?

The focus on citizenship in Pfister's paper reminded us of the (taken for granted) importance of the relationship that individual citizens have with the State in Western democracies. Citizenship, as a form of social contract, is what binds individuals to the state and vice versa. The concept is used extensively in debates about European social policy to frame discussions about agency, marginalisation and exclusion. How relevant are these debates to an understanding of malfunctioning health systems in Uganda? Might it be, for example, that the quality of these relationships, between Uganda as a State and its citizens, is a factor at least partially explaining the apparent 'demotivation' of healthcare workers? Indeed, could some of the behaviour characterised as demotivation or disinterest (or even limited individual capacity) be otherwise conceptualised as 'social struggles on the ground.' A form of civil disobedience: perhaps a rational response to marginalisation and oppression? (2012: 244). Or, what Kostakopoulou refers to as 'tactical subjectivity' (cited in Pfister 2012: 245).

It is interesting to take a step back here and consider the role that the National Health Service (NHS) plays in the UK not just in the provision of health care but also in symbolising the relationship between citizens and the State. The NHS (in common with the Ugandan health service) is a universal public service, free at the point of use. However, for the time being the NHS remains the sector of choice for the majority. The Ugandan system, on the other hand, is a residualised (ineffective) safety net for the poorest people who have no choice and no means to access private services. Even the majority of Ugandan healthcare workers would not use the services they provide. In this context, it is 'easier' to categorise the system and the patients who use it as 'other' or even as the 'undeserving poor' (Marshall 1950).

Environment is not then a disconnected or disembodied 'given' facilitating or obstructing individual choices in the public health environment. It is itself constituted through social interaction: 'law, political institutions, the economy and technology are always created, interpreted and endowed with meaning through social interaction [ ... ] they are human constructions influencing our agency' (Pfister, 248).

We have noted that this work is primarily theoretical. However, it is interesting to note Pfister's reflections on the methodological implications of these approaches. He suggests that the majority of 'empirical operationalisations' of the CA approach are quantitative, 'drawing on aggregative data, indices and statistics' (p. 251) and necessarily retrospective. In conclusion, he advocates complementing CA with 'qualitative interaction-oriented' dimensions to 'investigate human beings as creators of the world they inhabit' (p. 252).

The work reviewed earlier introduces a variety of complex concepts to an understanding of health worker behaviour. What is most interesting is the weighting attached to context and the emphasis on employment and the *quality of work*. The clinical focus and epistemology underpinning the behavioural science approach has the (unintended) effect of drawing us away from the obvious: that understanding the behaviour of health workers in low-resource settings is fundamentally about work and not health as such. Moving on from the concept of capabilities, we also began to feel uneasy about the (apparently highly individualised) concept of 'motivation' in behavioural science and how it sat alongside our experiences of Ugandan health workers. Coupled with the emphasis on labour markets in Barbard's paper, this led us to return to and widen our knowledge of the literature on HRM or the more specialist sub-field identified as 'human resources for health.'[9]

## FINDING COMMONALITY? PERSPECTIVES FROM HUMAN RESOURCE MANAGEMENT (HRM)

What the world wants is a good job. That is one of the biggest discoveries Gallup has ever made. It is the single most dominant thought carried around in the heads of most people . . . it establishes our relationships with our city, our country, and the whole world around us (Clifton 2007: 3).

Social science, and perhaps research in general, has a tendency to seek out the abnormal or exotic unintentionally glossing over the mundane everyday commonality that unites rather than distinguishes us. This quote from a Gallup survey underlines the most obvious but often overlooked issue that lies at the core of health worker motivation. It does not provide all the answers or angles but it presents a sound universalising, rather than essentialising, starting point from which we can begin to understand context and diversity.

There is a lively and burgeoning corpus of research focusing on health worker motivation from what can be loosely described as 'human resource management' (HRM) perspectives. Buchan, with reference to the UK context, argues that 'the importance of the management of human resources to the success or failure of health sector reform has often been overlooked' (2000; 319). Interestingly a review of a large number of papers from a range of international contexts suggests a powerful commonality of 'drivers' in diverse low- and high-resource settings. The work by Nzinga et al. on the implementation of guidelines in Kenyan hospitals concludes that 'the barriers identified are broadly the same in theme to those reported from high-income settings' (2009: 1).

One of the things that distinguish the HRM approach from behavioural science is the concept of 'motivation.' As noted earlier, behavioural science tends to treat motivation as an intrinsic variable: internal to the individual. In a recent presentation on behavioural science approaches and their potential contribution to understanding behaviour change in global health, Byrne-Davis argued that 'when we as behavioural scientists talk about motivation it is very moment to moment [ . . . ] motivation [is about] automatic reflexes; about what we're going to do – a kind of in the moment reflex' (presentation to the THET Patient Safety Program meeting, November 2015).

The HRM literature centrestages motivation but the key to motivation lies not with intrinsic individual attributes but organisational contexts: it is relational and in some contexts disproportionately extrinsic. In this model, the structural/organisational context lies at the heart not the periphery of behaviour change. The study by Nzinga et al. is interesting as it positions itself within the behavioural science spectrum as an example of evidence-based medicine (2009: 1). However, the qualitative approach utilised (interviews) generates a whole range of findings, nearly all of which are focused on local contextual conditions and weaknesses in HRM. It is perhaps no surprise that they conclude that, 'Future research might benefit from the disciplines of organisational management as well as behavioural sciences' (2009: 8).

The organisational focus characteristic of HRM theories tends to define motivation quite narrowly as 'an individual's degree of willingness to exert and maintain an effort *towards organisational goals*' (Dieleman et al. 2006: 2). The emphasis on the organisation is further exemplified in the definition of HRM offered by Mathauer and Imhoff: 'Human Resource Management is the management of people in **an** organisation' (2006: 4). Having said that, Mathauer and Imhoff (2006) take a broader view of motivational dynamics suggesting that 'Health workers are demotivated and frustrated precisely because they are unable to satisfy their professional conscience' (2006: 1). This latter approach certainly resonates better with our experiences in Uganda perhaps because of the sheer lack of effective and tangible HRM in most (dysfunctional) facilities. The views of the following Ugandan health worker suggest an identification of himself as a professional rather than as an employee (although the issues he raises pertain to wider aspects of resource management):

> Poor working conditions means you have the knowledge but people are dying in your hands. Emotionally, professionally, you feel you should not be in that area. For us health workers we feel touched when these people die in our hands yet we know we could have saved their lives if 1, 2, 3 things were in place. And we know it is possible to put them in place but somebody somewhere has not put them in place. So, as a professional, when people are dying in your hands because you don't have some of the things to help them and you know what to do – you feel you should not be in that place actually – you feel those people shouldn't come to you (UHW).

Khan and Ackers (2004) critique the 'unitarist' perspectives of what they term 'Western HRM' advocating a more pluralist approach capable of 'institutionalising some elements of the "African social system" into formal

HRM policies and strategies' (2004: 1330). They are not referring so much here to multiple employment or systems within systems (i.e. corruption) but more to the role of 'normative stakeholders' such as extended family clans and religious brotherhoods. In the Ugandan context, tribal affiliation plays an important role both within existing organisations and as external, inter-locking organisations. Tribal affiliations also compete with and lie in some tension with national and organisational identities. For now the main point here is that viewing motivation from the perspective of 'the' single employ-ing organisation may be far too narrow.

The following section summarises some of the key findings reproduced in a selection of papers on health worker motivation.[10] There is a strong tendency to distinguish financial from non-financial variables. Whilst, unsurprisingly, especially in low-income settings, pay is a key driver of health worker motivation, it is by no means the only or even the most important factor. Pay emerges most powerfully for less-well-paid cadres where pay is currently below subsistence level; it is impossible to maintain a basic quality of life through full-time public employment. This is the case in Uganda for most cadres of staff. A typical nurse or midwife in Uganda earns between 400,000 and 800,000 Ugandan shillings a month (£100–£170) depending on levels of qualification.[11] Length of service continues to have a major influence on pay in Uganda, despite its discriminatory consequences.[12] This reduces incentives for individual investment in career development.

A further complication arises due to administrative inefficiency and poor financial governance resulting in health workers often not being paid at all for months. Doctors (and specialists) are generally less likely to stress pay as a key motivating factor no doubt because they are able to top-up their wages through private work (as noted in Chapter 2). The qualitative research by Mathauer and Imhoff on non-financial incentives acknowledges the importance of financial incentives, 'especially in those situations where income is insufficient to meet even the most basic needs of health professionals and their families'. [However] 'Increased salaries are by no means sufficient to solve the problem of low motivation . . . More money does not imply more motivation' (2006: 2). Indeed, and unsur-prisingly if we reflect on our own experiences as employees,[13] issues like security, leadership, recognition, clear understandings of roles and work-loads, equitable access to opportunities for professional and career devel-opment, equality, autonomy, participation and access to the resources essential for effective work (consumables, equipment and medicines etc.) are all frequently cited (Fig. 4.3).

> Lack of **leadership** (poor role models) and supportive management: lack of active engagement in development of organisational goals
>
> Lack of collaborative and inter-professional decision making & **team working** (hierarchy and disrespect especially from doctors) contributes to the development of a culture in which knowledge is not valued or shared (envy and isolation)
>
> Overwhelming **workloads** and lack of workload management compounded by endemic absenteeism (see below).
>
> Poor **communication**
>
> Lack of **recognition** and appreciation (blame culture)
>
> Absence of 'open recruitment' (**meritocratic and transparent**)
>
> Lack of clear **Role Descriptions** (especially for task-shifting cadres)
>
> Lack of **Performance Review/Appraisal** systems: lack of incentives and lack of disciplinary action/enforcement
>
> Lack of **career development**/progression opportunities (career ladders)
>
> Lack of /unfair access to **continuing professional development** resource
>
> Poor working environment, **working conditions,** infrastructure (lack of equipment, consumables and drugs) due to resource shortages and endemic corruption
>
> Fears about **personal safety and health**
>
> The pervasive influence of **systemic corruption** at all levels
>
> Daily challenges to **professionalism; the** inability to work effectively and witnessing the immediate consequences of that.

**Fig. 4.3** Non-financial human resource variables influencing health worker motivation in low-resource settings (*Source*: Authors' summary of reviewed HRM literature)

There is insufficient scope in this chapter to discuss these components of HRM in any detail. A clear message emerges that the health systems crisis in many low-resource settings is conceptualised as a crisis in human resource management and not inadequate capabilities per se. Indeed, Mbindyo et al. conclude their study (in concordance with BehSci theories) with the following statement:

> Interventions that aim to change worker practice simply by offering training are likely to fare poorly unless attention is paid to those factors influencing the motivation of health workers to change and perform well at individual, organisational and system levels (2009: 9).

According to the HRM model, the quality of the work environment (i.e. extrinsic factors) determines health worker motivations and poor performance/outcomes. It is the lack of congruence between individual goals (which may derive from their training, education, experience and professionalism), the goals of the organisation they are employed by and their ability to achieve these goals that impacts motivation.

From a methods point of view, it is interesting to note that the HRM work reviewed here is quite eclectic, often drawing on multi-disciplinary perspectives. And, most of the papers reviewed are based on in-depth qualitative research in the field. Mbindyo et al., for example, argue that qualitative methods are necessary 'to explore the depth, richness, and complexity of staff motivation' (2009: 2).

## Perspectives from Evolutionary Economics

At this point in our 'journey' we came across, quite by chance (or serendipity), another body of work. We had in fact worked in collaboration with Carolina Cañibano,[14] an economist, for some years (on research careers) and it was while searching for a paper linked to that work that we came across a publication with the term 'capabilities' in the title. On initial reading we realised that, despite the complexity of its theoretical underpinnings[15] and language and entirely different context, this new area of work (to us) had surprising relevance to the work we had been doing in Uganda.

Their work is presented as a critique of economic theories, including neoclassical and neo-Darwinian theories which fail, in the authors' views, to capture the role played by 'purposeful human action'. The same critique could be levelled at the concept of 'automatic behaviour' represented in the COM-b model.

Along with most of the evolutionary economics literature and the contributions to the discussion on capabilities from organisational and management studies, this work is targeted on innovation processes taking place within organisations with an implicit focus on the context of the 'firm' (i.e. private, market-oriented, for-profit, organisations) and economic systems change. One might question the relevance of this framework set within the context of 'knowledge economies' to an understanding of the role of professional voluntarism in public health systems in Uganda. At face value, the diversity of context and language may suggest that opportunities for policy transfer are minimal. Again, a systematic review would have screened this kind of work out.

However, if we can see beyond this diversity, core commonalities emerge.

With reference to scientific mobility, Kuvic defines 'productivity' and 'innovation' in a way that appears immediately relevant:

> Productivity is about the quality of work produced. Innovation entails specialised knowledge or creativity that is 'less easily measured' and the output is also based on the level of motivation of the individual. It is essential that employers build an environment in the workforce that can foster this type of work (2015: 16).

If we take the view that low-resource settings (such as Uganda) are also part of the global knowledge economy, conceptualise health systems change in terms of innovation and health workers as economic actors (within these systems) and the logic of understanding health worker outcomes in terms of 'productivity', then the relevance is clear. Indeed, we would argue that using this form of language allows us to avoid the risks of essentialising health worker behaviour in low-resource settings (capabilities and motivations) and emphasising the core commonalities between firms in high-resource settings and public health organisations (in both high- and low-resource settings). The language of innovation and entrepreneurship is also far more positive and aspirational.

The following section distils some of the key concepts and processes represented in the work of these economists enabling us to identify the links with the theories discussed earlier and the potential for more holistic, multi-disciplinary, theoretical underpinnings to support the deployment of professional volunteers in health systems change.

Muñoz et al. (2011) propose an 'action plan framework' to focus on the theoretical concept of intentionality. Intentionality, that is, the dynamics of goals formation towards which agents direct their action, plays a major role in driving economic change. In pursuing their intended goals agents activate learning and the potential for new knowledge combinations emerges. This is the key mechanism for the evolution of capabilities. In addition, goals may be of different sorts. Agents (read health workers) may conceive highly transformative goals and direct their action towards new imagined realities but they may also formulate action plans with poor transformational potential. To account for this qualitative difference between types of action goals, the authors define 'innovative intentionality' as 'the will to conceive or imagine realities with the purpose of making them effective' (Cañibano et al. 2006: 319). Economic agents, as individuals or organisations, can in turn be qualified as operating with higher or lower levels of innovative intentionality. This approach and the weighting given to *intentionality as the key driver* can be contrasted both with the behavioural science model and, as Muñoz et al. explain, with the economic literature which, 'argues that knowledge is the only foundation of capabilities' (2011: 194). For Muñoz et al., economic evolution (systemic change) does not come about as a result of the growth of knowledge per se. Intention, not capability, is the starting point.

The concepts that immediately captured our imagination and resonated most starkly with our experience in Uganda included the explicit engagement with agency and the emphasis the model places on existing knowledge. Learning is not something that *happens to* people as passive actors/victims (or empty vessels) but something that is essentially relational, interactive and cumulative. The individuals concerned are not devoid of (or lacking in) knowledge per se; indeed, it is their experiential (tacit and highly contextualised) knowledge – 'their perceived realities' – that shapes their response to new learning and imported knowledge. Agency is explicitly recognised in this model, which assumes that 'humans have sufficient intelligence and incentives to anticipate and avoid the selection effects' associated with evolutionary, Darwinian theories (Muñoz et al. 2011: 194 citing; Witt 2004: 128).

This approach to intentionality helps us to see motivation as contextualised and as much about extrinsic as it is about intrinsic factors. In the first instance, health workers are heterogeneous and this heterogeneity is 'not only a matter of differences in knowledge [or innate ability], but also of differences in action goals and intentions' (Cañibano et al. 2006: 319) and their subjective responses to means (opportunities) or plans will shape their approach to new learning. Furthermore, a health worker's motivation will vary over time and space and in relation to diverse plans. A person, according to this model, cannot be placed on a linear motivation–demotivation or innate intelligence continuum: their degree of motivation will necessarily vary according to specific plans (places, conditions and relationships). Seeing motivation as fundamentally context-driven helpfully removes some of the essentialising (and potentially racist) elements of the behavioural science model.

Although Muñoz and Encinar (2014a) locate their paper within the paradigm of innovation systems and speak of knowledge-based economies and 'firms' their point that 'the systemic properties of the system emerge as a result of agent interaction' (2014a: 72) appear just as relevant to an understanding of public healthcare systems. The system is as it is (and is subject to change through) the interaction of agents operating at multi-levels (from the Ministry of Health, through District Health Authorities, tribal boundaries and down to health facilities and individual health workers employed within them).

Whilst similar concepts are identified in the work discussed before, the 'action plan' model places unique emphasis on intentionality (the intention to do something) and conceptualises it as part of action planning or goal setting. It is this intentionality and planning that drives the process and activates learning and not the other way around (albeit in a constantly iterative and reflexive process).

The (subjective) process of planning so central to this approach is informed by deeply localised knowledge of the opportunities and constraints open to individual agents. The concept of 'information stocks' by Muñoz et al. (2011: 198) captures for us the importance of recognising pre-existing contextualised knowledge *as* knowledge and not simply lack of interest/demotivation. This may take the form of explicit, experiential knowledge (of delivering countless dead babies, for example[16]) and/or tacit knowledge (defined here as know-how,[17] skills, competencies, routines, capacities, capabilities' (Muñoz et al. 2011: 312).

Rather than the lack of knowledge it could be the sheer weight (grinding heaviness) of tacit knowledge that influences attitudes to new learning. Arguably, it is precisely this knowledge that newly arriving professional volunteers lack, limiting their own ability to formulate innovative knowledge re-combinations that restrict progress. It is not to say that the cutting-edge clinical expertise they bring is not of value but needs time (and humility) to settle and recombine with local knowledge in order to identify effective and sustainable and contextualised interventions. As Williams and Balatz (2008a) assert, this kind of knowledge travels less easily and requires co-presence.

This model doesn't privilege new learning and helps to explain how new learning (introduced by professional volunteers) must be seen to work in combination with existing knowledge (rather than displacing it). Echoing the work of Williams and Balatz (2008a) and Polanyi (1959), Muñoz et al. suggest that a significant proportion of organisational and individual knowledge is tacit (2011: 312) and yet when professional volunteers and development organisations intervene in low-resource settings they tend to focus on training in explicit (clinical) skills and, in the process, assume that the failure to behave in certain ways is a reflection of the absence of knowledge rather than the presence of it and its impact on health workers' perceived reality.

'Action planning' is described by Muñoz et al. as the 'analytic unit connecting means/actions and goals' (2011: 195). And connections play a very central role in this model: 'Agencies (individuals and organisations) make plans and planning implies making connections' (p. 196). It is the 'recombinant process of connections' that may generate what the authors term 'novelties'.[18] The concept of connections here goes beyond a narrow definition of connections as social capital (networks and contacts) to embrace the boundary spanning /brokering qualities of knowledge itself. This fits with the authors' assertion that 'learning consists of testing (and eventually retaining) new connections that prove useful for agents to reach their goals' (p. 196).

Furthermore, imagination plays a central role in action planning. The concept of 'imagined realities' resonates powerfully with our work with Ugandan health workers and captures perfectly the dynamics of their highly contextualised situations. *Is it possible in the context within which Ugandan health workers are placed to imagine a different reality?*

Muñoz and Encinar (2014b) point out that economic processes (systems) are historical and action planning by agents takes place in a context of 'radical uncertainty' (p. 319). In that sense planning is not an objective, linear, exercise but a reflexive, subjective and uncertain process.

The fundamentally subjective quality of the concept of perceived/ imagined realities, coupled with the acknowledgement of existing deeply experiential and localised knowledge (as knowledge rather than the absence of it), enable us to understand the equally important concept of 'bounded rationality' (Simon 1985; Jones 1999) employed by these authors. Behaviour (or the lack of it) that may be interpreted by the outsider observer (a professional volunteer, for example, or clinical 'expert') as irrational or unproductive may, when understood in context, be rational (a new reality may not be possible).

The 'action plan' model identifies the importance of 'means,' conceptually equivalent to the 'opportunities' represented in the behavioural science model, and an implicit component of context and perceived realities. Conceptually it is present but underspecified in what is essentially a theoretical model. This is an area where the HRM research coupled with our own contextual knowledge can add flesh to the conceptual bones (framework). The fact that the economics model was not specifically designed to 'fit' the context to which we are now seeking to apply it perhaps explains this lack of specificity which, in the case of the Ugandan health system, will have profound effects on its application.[19] This is captured poignantly by Muñoz et al. as a 'dialectical dance between feasibility and desirability' (Muñoz et al. 2011: 198). Health workers, as agents, evaluate and formulate their plans in the context of their own experience of what works.

Cañibano et al. (citing Teece et al. 2000) define 'dynamic capabilities' as 'the ability to reconfigure, redirect, transform, and appropriately shape and integrate existing core competences with external resources and strategic and complementary assets to achieve new and innovative forms of competitive advantage' (2006: 313). Furthermore, the process of acquiring or developing dynamic capabilities is a 'collective learning process from which an organisation improves its ability to achieve its goals' (p. 313).

The reference here to learning as a collective process is interesting from the perspective of professional voluntarism and health partnership activity where learning, whether in the classroom or in one-to-one mentoring, is almost always seen and planned as an individual process (taking person X from point A to B along a continuum of measurable (quantifiable) learning outcomes. It would be interesting to assess whether developing more active forms of learning focused on collectives[20] (multi-disciplinary teams within facilities) and working with their imagined realities may activate learning and improve outcomes.

It is the interaction of intentions and action goals that drive the evolution of 'dynamic capabilities'. Capabilities in this model are certainly not reducible to genetic (inherited) capacities (such as intelligence). Rather they are informed by existing knowledge and constantly reshaped.

Intentionality linked to goals is what 'activates the development of capabilities, the testing of new connections within a system, and, therefore, the generation of new knowledge' (Muñoz and Encinar 2014a: 75).

The 'action plan' model presents learning as a (hyper-)active process involving the 're-combination'[21] of new knowledge with existing explicit and tacit knowledge. Muñoz and Encinar describe intentions as 'triggering [ ... ] driven learning processes' configuring connections which give rise to evolving capabilities. (2014a: 75). In the language of evolutionary economics, these may stimulate 'entrepreneurial experimentation'. The reference to the creation of 'new genetic material' (p. 76) represents an interesting challenge to the more essentialising tendencies of behaviour science and classical economics, which assume that genetics are fixed and determine capabilities (or are the same thing).

Ultimately, innovative intentionality is the activator of constantly and reflexively evolving 'action plans' that interact with 'social reality' to drive transformative change. Of course, such change is not always wholly or even partially effective: the authors accept the possibility that planned action may fail to lead to intended outcomes as a result of unintended consequences or externality effects (Muñoz and Encinar 2014b: 318).

As noted earlier, this area of work is entirely driven by theory and remains untested in any empirical context. This in part explains its luxuriousness and ability to deal with complexity.[22]

## A SYNTHETIC, MULTI-DISCIPLINARY APPROACH?

Echoing the conclusions of Nzinga et al. (2009), Muñoz et al. conclude that Understanding human behaviour lies at the 'frontier of economics and psychology' (2011: 317 citing Brocas and Carillo 2004). Indeed, all of the authors reviewed here advocate the need for multi-disciplinary approaches even if they themselves resist the challenge. Having reviewed the approaches in the context of our much grounded action-research on professional voluntarism, we feel that the model that best fits the situation is that represented by the SI Framework.

We are particularly attracted by the attention the economic 'action plan' approach pays to existing knowledge or 'information banks' and the effect this knowledge has on perceptions of what reality is and could be. We feel that this theory helps us to understand why so many interventions fail. Knowledge does not activate change: rather intentions organised through plans (and agency) drive and activate learning. And new learning builds connections between people and knowledge to create the conditions in which change can begin to be imagined and actioned. The emphasis on the collective and connected quality of active learning is also very helpful and encourages us to see beyond learning as an individualised process.

Having said that all the models share broad ideas, each one discusses individual behaviour in some form of structure-agency/choice-constraint framework. Each recognises the importance of tacit knowledge. Each refers to motivation and to goals or plans in some shape or form and to opportunities or resources and each pays some attention to multi-level contexts. The capabilities approach is focused primarily on supranational and national systems using the concept of citizenship to describe the relationship between individuals (as citizens) and the state. The state is important but we must see this as multi-level too and, in the Ugandan case, transected by other critical elements of identity, belonging and political affiliation: tribes remain of great importance, brokering the kinds of citizenship relationships identified in the European Union. Schaaf and Freedman's work on health worker posting emphasises the importance of recognising that the 'state' is not a unified or necessarily benevolent actor but reflects many conflicting interests and norms that shape individual and organisational behaviour (2015: 7).

With the exception of HRM, all of the approaches tend to gloss over the organisational context, which plays a vital intermediary function. Only HRM theory really captures the everyday reality of employment relations and the quality of work. However, it tends to perhaps over-emphasise 'the organisation' and the impact of employer–employee relations on wider motivational dynamics. Many employees in Uganda and elsewhere will move between employers or (as is very common) have more than one job. The reference to professionalism illustrates the notion that a person's identity and sense of responsibility may not always align first and foremost with a particular employer. Indeed, doctors in Uganda (and elsewhere) often identify themselves with their profession more than a specific health facility that pays what is in most cases a tiny fraction of their overall income. International organisations (NGOs and health partnerships) may also be important organisational actors here perhaps interfacing with local employing organisations (such as the SVP) or directly with individual health workers (through salary top-ups or moonlighting).

Certainly it is widely recognised that individual employers play only a partial role in contemporary career planning. Perhaps reflecting its empirical strengths (and grounding in qualitative research) the HRM literature is important to our work not so much because of its theoretical contribution but the attention to detailed analysis of employment quality that resonates so sharply with our own understanding of Ugandan health worker's experiences. This level of analysis has supported our ability to design very practical evidence-based interventions.

This concept of bounded rationality (in the economic model) is perhaps far more relevant than the architects of these papers anticipated. One of the limitations of the papers, perhaps reflecting the level of abstraction, is the lack of attention to conflict and power: the possibility of multiple realities and parallel organisational cultures. Corruption is systemic in Uganda especially within the public sector; it can be described as a culture. It is pervasive and starts from the very top of organisations and the systems within which they are based and operates through powerful, organised syndicates. Health workers (and patients) are acutely aware of its existence, the personal benefits that derive from it and the profound risks associated with challenging it. It is interesting to note the reference by Muñoz et al. to the entrepreneur as a 'destabilising agent' (2011: 199). 'Destabilising' in this context could imply creative disruption triggering innovation (in the right direction). Alternatively, or simultaneously, it could refer to the impact of corruption. This detailed (tacit and explicit) knowledge of how corruption works at every level and in every decision necessarily shapes both imagined realities and action plans. In this sense, there may be two parallel systems operating in marked tension with each other within a health facility or authority. Chapter 3 has discussed the impact of corruption on professional volunteers and their relationships with Uganda health workers identifying the dynamics of power and hierarchy (positionalities). None of the theories reviewed pays explicit attention to these dimensions of context. Interestingly it is often the lack of knowledge on the part of foreign agencies and individual volunteers rather than their superior clinical knowledge that limits impact and generates unintended consequences.[23] Of course, corruption pollutes not only organisations but also the wider system that nurtures it, fundamentally weakening a sense of identity with the state at national or local level and also with 'leaders' (at every level).

Whilst we can identify closely with the concept of 'action planning' as a vehicle for the exercise of individual agency based on the recombination of disparate knowledges, we have some concerns that the emphasis in the material reviewed, perhaps reflecting the business/private sector context, fails to explain inaction or stasis. Or, situations when human action, qua rational, as Muñoz and Encinar (2014a: 75) put it, could amount to non-decisions or inaction. On a practical level, it may prove impossible to imagine returns on an investment (in training, for example, or even coming to work regularly). Equally (and commonly) the risks associated and predicted (as a component of perceived reality) may lead a person to consciously decide not to challenge a corruption syndicate or even show some initiative. Indeed, we have seen a number of innovative individuals motivated to formulate plans which activate new learning and bring about systems change effectively punished and threatened by their peers and their line managers for stepping out of line. Simply being seen with 'muzungus' leads to perceptions of financial gain and ensuing envy followed by punishment. Just as the association of 'immobility' with competitiveness has been challenged (Ferro 2006), inactivity needs to be seen as rational in certain contexts.

## CONCLUSION

The research review work that formed the basis of this chapter was entered into following our growing realisation grounded in evidence gained from in-depth qualitative research, that many if not most of the interventions utilising professional volunteers as knowledge brokers have largely failed to generate visible and sustainable impact on health systems. Or, put more simply, training Ugandan health workers has failed to translate into evidence of individual behaviour change. The exploration of other research marked an attempt to answer the 'why' question and, if necessary change our methods of intervention.

All of the approaches reviewed here offer important insights and we would not wish to privilege any disciplinary or theoretical approach but rather to identify those aspects that we feel are most applicable. Recent studies applying the COM-B model to an evaluation of behaviour change in CPD interventions in low-resource settings concluded that 'None of capability, opportunity or motivation were found to predict either behaviour or behavioural intention' (Byrne-Davis et al. 2016: 68). The authors suggest that this may reflect the fact that the validation of these tools took place in 'resource-rich, high-income environments' which may 'reduce the applicability of some behaviour change theories to this [low resource] context'. Having said that, the other theories reviewed here have not attempted empirical verification remaining at 'ideas' stage.

Our empirical work confirms the importance of the three components of the COM-B approach: namely of capabilities, opportunities and motivations. However, it rather turns the equation on its head suggesting (as SI theory proposes) that intentionality comes first: you have to be motivated to learn. And this motivation is not intrinsic but, and especially in low-resource settings, is fundamentally extrinsic and context bound. And, in that frame, local knowledge, especially tacit knowledge of what works and can even be imagined to work, drives motivation. So knowledge can act as a break on individual intentions (if we have learnt repeatedly that plans or interventions do not work or cause us personal risk/harm).

Chapter 5 builds on the material presented in this and previous chapters to reflect on the learning that has taken place since we began to deploy professional volunteers to Uganda. Perhaps unusually at this stage in a book, it organises this reflection around two empirical case studies. These are used to illustrate the iterative quality of our evidence-based interventions and the role that research has played in taking us to the conclusion that the primary learning is learning from failure and not quantifying success.

## NOTES

1. Serendipity or happenchance has been increasingly recognised as important sources of social capital in research (Ackers and Gill 2008).
2. Epistemology is defined in the *Oxford Dictionary* as 'the theory of knowledge, especially with regard to its methods, validity, and scope, and the distinction between justified belief and opinion'.
3. COMb stands for Capabilities, Opportunities, Motivation and Behaviour.
4. www.vichealth.vic.gov.au/cochrane.
5. An example of how this approach can be applied to the evaluation of health partnership interventions can be seen in Jones et al. (2013).
6. The authors then developed a complex scientific tool incorporating a Delphi-style consensus process and a range of 'open and closed sort tasks' and 'fuzzy cluster analysis' as the basis for the refinement of the TDF.
7. This definition of motivation as 'processes in the brain that energise and direct behaviour' is taken directly from Robert Wests' PRIME Theory (2006). It is important to point out that PRIME theory was developed in the context of alcohol and drug addiction in the UK and not health worker behaviour.
8. See Guardian http://www.theguardian.com/politics/2013/apr/08/margaret-thatcher-quotes.
9. This is the title of a journal which captures a lot of this material.

10. As noted, the objective of this chapter is not to present a comprehensive literature review across all disciplines. Our aim has been to identify work which we feel 'speaks to' our objectives and has the potential to contribute to the evidence base informing our interventionsevidence base informing our interventions. This section reviews the following papers: Buchan (2000: 2004); Chen et al. (2004); Chopra et al. (2008); Dieleman et al. (2006); Franco et al. 2002); Mangham and Hanson (2008); Mathauer and Imhoff (2006); Mbindyo et al. (2009); Nzinga et al. (2009); Stringhini et al. (2009); Willis-Shattuck et al. (2008).

11. Our estimation of the level of income required in Kampala to meet basic subsistence needs (housing, food and school fees) for a family with two children is around 2 million Ugandan shillings (about £500 a month).

12. Seniority-based pay is explicitly prohibited as discriminatory under European Union employment law.

13. Similar findings came out of a study on pay and remuneration in research in the UK (Ackers et al. 2006).

14. We are very grateful for the opportunity to present a version of this chapter to Dr Cañibano's group in Valencia and to have received her insightful comments on this chapter.

15. Helfat and Peteraf (2009) suggest the level of complexity in the SI framework may have generated some confusion even within the field.

16. Ugandan health workers will have considerably more hands-on experience of many obstetric complications than their professional volunteer counterparts.

17. Gebauer refers to this as 'procedural knowledge' as distinct from 'declarative knowledge' (2012: 59).

18. The concept of 'novelties' is new to us and at first seemed rather strange. If we understand this as meaning new ideas or innovations it works well in the context of our work. Muñoz and Encinar define novelties as 'new realities' (2014b: 319).

19. Muñoz et al. do refer specifically to monetary and non-monetary elements of action plans echoing a core distinction in the HRM literature (2011: 195).

20. The concept of the 'collective understanding of knowledge' through 'assimilative learning' is also referred to by Gebauer et al. (2012).

21. This echoes Williams and Balatz's (2008a) reference to knowledge combinations discussed in Chapter 2.

22. Muñoz and Encinar point to criticisms that the SI approach is in fact 'overtheorised'.

23. In practice, this is a difficult but necessary component of induction processes and may be a factor to take into account when considering the efficacy of length of stay.

# Iterative Learning: 'Knowledge for Change'?

**Abstract** Chapter 5 applies the knowledge discussed in Chapter 4 to two illustrative case studies. Many interventions tend to represent a simple 'trial and error' approach underpinned by intensive grounded research to facilitate our understanding of change processes or change resistance. Tracking the identification of a 'need' and our experience of designing and monitoring the evaluation of that process, in the light of the new knowledge gained through ongoing research review, improves our understanding of the complexity of social processes. Chapter 5 redefines the objectives of our action-research project from setting out to capture the ingredients of positive change to pro-actively understanding and learning from failure. It attempts, in the context of this potentially debilitating reality, to take stock and identify the characteristics of least-harm interventions to chart the next stage of our journey.

It concludes with a series of recommendations aimed at policy makers and volunteer deployment agencies.

**Keywords** Complex interventions · Intervention failure · Corruption · Knowledge deficit model

© The Author(s) 2017                                                           113
H.L. Ackers, J. Ackers-Johnson, *Mobile Professional Voluntarism and International Development*, DOI 10.1057/978-1-137-55833-6_5

## INTRODUCTION: UNDERSTANDING FAILURE
## IN COMPLEX INTERVENTIONS

Chapter 5 takes stock of the material presented in the previous chapters and the cumulative knowledge gained from 8 years' experience of intensive action-oriented evaluation research. Our learning and 'knowing' as activists and researchers has been a continuous process: there was no point at which we went into the field knowledge or value-free and we have and will never reach the point of knowledge saturation (ultimate truth). Research of this nature is a journey. Perhaps the greatest single quality of any researcher (or volunteer) embarking on this type of journey is the honesty and humility to accept that we are always learning and also that, in many respects, we are not simply (or usually) measuring positive outcomes but trying to understand intervention failure and inertia. This may not be the message individual researchers, volunteers or their funding bodies want to hear. However, observing and understanding policy failure does not imply failure on the part of the actors/projects concerned. Far from it. Indeed, a growing body of research documents the specific quality of higher-level entrepreneurial learning that arises from 'hard knocks' or 'discontinuous events' (Cope 2003, 2011). In a rather different context, Mayer suggests that errors present the learner with robust feedback that can act as scaffolding for future learning (2008) and Somekh identifies 'episodes of substantial friction' or 'knots' as starting points for deeper collaboration (2006: 23).

On a broader and more ethical note, interventions and associated research are not there to benefit individual actors, be they researchers, volunteers, projects, funding bodies or 'the industry' (Valters 2015), but rather to 'maximise the likelihood that knowledge generated will be ultimately of benefit to humanity' (Richards 2015: 3).

The Sustainable Volunteering Project (in common with other similar projects and probably most Health Partnership interventions) has very broad and ambitious objectives focused on systemic improvements in maternal and newborn health through professional voluntarism. This type of project is perhaps best characterised as an example of a 'complex intervention'. If we accept the UK Medical Research Council's definition of complex interventions as those involving 'several interacting components' (MRC 2008: 6) then, as Richards argue, 'simplicity is probably a chimera[1]' and most interventions should be considered as 'complex' (2015: 2). Richards clarifies this definition suggesting that complexity is not so much about the intervention itself but the questions we are posing. Where context is seen to be of great importance and where we are interested not so much in 'does' an intervention work but 'how' or 'why' it works (or perhaps how/why it does not work) then it must qualify as complex.

Furthermore, Hallberg argues that complexity is relevant when we are addressing interventions with several or multiple individual components and when considering how these interact with one another (2015: 17). According to these criteria, it is clear that the SVP qualifies as a 'complex intervention'. And that intervention comprises numerous constituent interventions that have emerged in a very iterative and reflexive way throughout the duration of the wider programme. The unplanned nature of these may indicate a lack of planning or element of what the MRC refers to somewhat dismissively as 'pragmatism' (2008: 9). We would rather contend that this represents a necessary commitment to democratic engagement and subsidiarity supporting grounded policy engagement and development. And, a degree of 'planned happenchance' (Malecki 2013: 87) or serendipity (Ackers and Gill 2008: 59) has been identified as a key component of social networking, creativity and entrepreneurialism.

The chapter opens with the presentation of two case studies illustrating the kinds of learning arising from the progressive failure of specific constituent interventions. The two cases are chosen as they represent generic/foundational 'back-to-basics' initiatives that lie at the heart of many, if not most, Health Partnership interventions in low-resource settings. For the purposes of this chapter we have adopted the approach advocated by the MRC for the evaluation of complex interventions. This involves identifying 'a theoretical understanding of the likely process of change'[2] (2008: 9); identifying outcomes and then, in a break from traditional experimental methods, assessing causal mechanisms and contextual factors.

## CASE STUDY 1: 'WAITING KILLS': CONGESTION, DISORDER AND PATIENT MANAGEMENT

The need for improved patient management is immediately evident on arrival in any large public health facility in Uganda. Stark visible evidence of over-crowding with patients and attendants on floors and spilling over into corridors and outdoor areas confronts and shocks every recently arrived professional volunteer. Similarly, every Ugandan health professional visiting a UK facility is immediately struck by the image of orderliness and effective patient management. Triage[3] is a foundational component of basic patient safety and underpins all subsequent clinical interventions (in that facility). It is perhaps no surprise that so many volunteers and HPs visiting Uganda have identified triage as a priority and sought to intervene.

*Initial 'Theory of Change': The Development of a More Structured System to Prioritise Patients According to Clinical Need Will Improve Clinical Interventions and Patient Outcomes.*

Case study 1 reports on a series of constituent interventions that together comprise a more composite and complex intervention. We have reported it here in a way that infers linearity. To some extent, the intervention did emerge over time in one facility becoming more complex and multi-faceted as the interventions progressively failed to impact and our knowledge of the context and failure dynamics deepened. However, similar interventions (with slight differences in approach reflecting the particular qualities of individual partnerships and institutional settings) all met with similar resistance and none has delivered sustained impact. In that respect, we are combining (rather loosely) a longitudinal and comparative case study approach.

In the first instance, and perhaps reflecting presumptions about roles and a profound belief in the value/logic of training (as noted in Chapter 3), a common starting point is typically the co-production/adaptation of protocols and associated short-course training.

*Intervention: Skills Deficits*
The identification of the 'problem' during the early phases of LMP intervention was that the failure to triage patients effectively is immediately and directly linked to skills deficits among Ugandan public health workers. In the language of behavioural science theories, we were focusing attention here on individual (clinical) **capabilities**. The operational *Theory of Change* at this point can be described as follows: Engagement of UK professional volunteers alongside Ugandan counterparts in the co-production of appropriate protocols and associated (CME) training and local awareness-raising will encourage effective patient triage.

At this stage, the intervention could be described as alarmingly simple involving the transmission of explicit clinical skills (how to do, record and interpret basic patient observations) in order to prioritise care. So simple, in fact, that our early interventions now look incredibly naive and must have been the source of much amusement on the part of local Ugandan managers.

Evaluation of this intervention is often achieved through straightforward 'measuring' tools recording the volume of staff trained, testing skills acquisition before-and-after CMEs and assessing subsequent implementation through (numerical) evidence of completion of observations in patient notes. We combined these (obligatory methods) with ongoing ethnographic fieldwork involving the project evaluator, the professional volunteers (as action-researchers), a dedicated social science volunteer and local collaborators.

**Outcomes**
Unfortunately, the outcomes associated with this form of intervention have been consistently disappointing. While it is common to recruit large numbers for CME training and to report strong evidence of initial skills acquisition among the cohort trained it is rare to see any evidence of sustained behaviour change. Limited short-term compliance is typically witnessed in defined areas (spaces/units) where volunteers involved in the intervention remain co-present for a period of time. Training in triage showed greater initial success in the 6-bed obstetric High Dependency Unit set up through LMP with funding support from THET. In many of the typical fly-in-fly-out CMEs where volunteer 'faculty' unfamiliar with the context leave immediately upon completion of training, implementation failure is unlikely to be recognised. Ongoing ethnographic observation combined with qualitative interviews and continual review of patient notes provided immediate evidence of impact failure and an emerging understanding of implementation gaps.

**Identifying and Responding to Failure**
In the initial stages of our intervention we were advised by local health workers that they were unable to use their new skills because they lacked resources, including stationary (for recording purposes) and basic equipment to take observations (stethoscopes and blood pressure machines, etc.). A review of parallel interventions in other settings (through literature and policy review work) identified similar outcomes and drew our attention to work on 'neglected processes'. At this point we held a workshop[4] in the UK inviting stakeholders from the UK and Ugandan arms of health partnerships

(plus a representative from the Ugandan Ministry of Health) to share experiences. The workshop achieved some consensus on problem definition and an ostensible commitment on the part of the MOH to prioritise, integrate and roll-out protocols (such as the African Maternal Early Warning Scoring System[5] or AMEWS). This failed to happen.

On the basis of expert advice, this led to a refined intervention involving the production of a personalised observation kit to be provided to every health worker in target locations with the aim of achieving a degree of saturation that would empower and motivate individuals to utilise their triage skills.

### Intervention: Physical Resource Deficits

The revised *Theory of Change* was focused on the opportunities that individuals (who have received the above training) have to utilise skills: providing personal observation kits would, we hoped, enable individuals to take observations in a timely fashion and empower/motivate them to do so. And, ensuring continuous supplies of stationary (by external organisations) will facilitate compliance. In the language of behavioural science theories, we were focusing attention here on individual (clinical) **opportunities**. Further complementary audit tools were co-developed (and discussed with health workers) to capture use of the kits and reduce the risks of theft/misuse.

### Outcomes

The intervention was a stark failure: outcomes associated with it were very limited with patchy and short-lived compliance. The co-presence of volunteers enhances compliance for the duration of their stay with almost immediate slippage once the volunteer leaves. Stationary remained a problem, especially in high-volume settings. The provision of personalised equipment failed to empower/motivate health workers and/or promote skills implementation. Personalised kits proved unsustainable even with audit systems in place.

### Identifying and Responding to Failure?

The approach proved to lack sustainability as the facility resisted demands to integrate the provision of stationary within the mainstream hospital system. Kits (as valuable commodities) were (very) favourably received and immediately utilised in zones where volunteers were actively present. However, equipment was 'lost' and the practice of using equipment suffered (very) rapid decline.[6]

*Intervention: Physical Resource Deficits (revised)*
A follow-up intervention negotiated with volunteers and senior line managers (who had it has to be said actively resisted the idea of providing personalised kits) involved 'permanently' affixing robust equipment and clocks to the walls of a dedicated triage area aimed to overcome the risks of theft and exploit the apparent benefits of establishing discrete and manageable 'zones'. This was supported by the institution of a simple and clear 'traffic light' system using colour-coded boxes affixed to the walls to prioritise patients: cases regarded as urgent were given a simple laminated red card. A US NGO later provided a high-tech electronic notice board to improve patient waiting, which soon after became dysfunctional.

**Outcomes**
Outcomes were initially strong with some excitement and pride in the new facility and equipment. However, compliance was short-lived. The co-presence of volunteers enhanced compliance for the duration of their stay only. Equipment became damaged and stolen almost immediately. The use of traffic light boxes became redundant as soon as the volunteer left; laminated red cards used to signify emergency cases mysteriously vanished. The continued (high volume) of staff rotations in this highly congested area made it harder to build cultural change and ensure a saturation level of training in the use of protocols.

**Identifying and Responding to Failure**
There was apparent confusion over the loss of equipment from the walls and disappearance of the laminated red cards (which have no monetary value). Confidential qualitative interviews with mid and senior facility managers (conducted off-site) revealed the presence of endemic and highly organised corruption 'syndicates'. They explained that triage (as prioritisation according to clinical need) lies in profound tension with organised and systemic corruption that is effectively smoke-screened through the appearance of chaos. The 'inert' knowledge deficit model fails to take account of in-depth local tacit knowledge (entrepreneurial destructive/confounding knowledge) impeding implementation. We learnt that chaos is planned and highly functional. It is also systemic: attempts to improve individual behaviour through investments in training (individual capabilities) and personalised equipment (opportunities) stood little chance of altering a system functioning effectively for many health workers and managers on the basis of corruption.

There is insufficient scope here to discuss corruption in more detail (see Ackers 2014). It is important to note however that corruption not only impacts local health workers and their ability to imagine new realities but also has a major impact on volunteer deployment and impact. The following example provided by a Ugandan health worker who had worked alongside SVP volunteers is illustrative:

> There is a problem with Ugandan midwives (working with volunteers). I've seen it. They think, 'oh she is white she will know what to do – she can do it by herself'. There is a problem of attitude amongst us – bad attitudes which give off a bad signal. I was in [a health facility] doing a delivery with a white volunteer and there was a retained placenta and oh my goodness the local midwife made a noise in her own language. She wanted money from the patient. She didn't want the white lady there so I said, 'you know what, let's go to another patient.'
> [Would the midwife try to get money from a patient even at the point at which she had a retained placenta?]
> Yes, of course. They are opportunists. They will look and think, 'behind that curtain that patient has nice bedsheets' so she won't want the volunteer there (UHW).

The very stark conclusion we have come to is that triage will fundamentally fail to work effectively in most (larger and congested) Ugandan public facilities where accountability is absent and efforts by volunteers to support it will be met by marked resistance: triage as a method of sorting patients according to clinical need lies in immediate tension with the sorting of patients according to their ability to pay.

Adherence to basic protocols (and in particular the AMEWS) was initially stronger in the dedicated 'High Dependency Unit' set up by the LMP charity with support from THET. This unit had only six beds and (necessarily) higher staffing levels. Equipment in such a confined space was less likely to be lost/stolen as greater accountability was in place. It was also easier to ensure a constant supply of stationary (via project funding). However, even in this more controlled setting, whilst the act of taking and documenting observations was more common, the logic of this process is that once certain critical points in the protocol are reached a doctor must be called. Midwifery staff were failing to 'escalate' care and call doctors when critical observations were recorded. Ethnographic work *in situ* combined with confidential qualitative interviews revealed unwillingness and, in some cases, fear of following this through. In practice, the staff either could not/would not use their own mobile phones for this process (at their own cost[7]) or had grown tired of repeated fruitless attempts to contact on-call doctors. In (many) other cases, midwives had experienced heavy criticism/chastisement from doctors for disturbing them. This is an endemic problem in Ugandan public health facilities.

Our analysis of failure at this stage illustrates the importance of combining explicit clinical skills with tacit knowledge and an emerging understanding of the impact of hierarchy and power (positionality) on relationships and implementation. We are no longer dealing with individuals but with complex organisations and 'systems within systems' founded on subversive knowledge rather than a lack of knowledge per se.

*Intervention: Human Resource System Deficits*
Continued CME training provided by volunteers and local staff was introduced to manage (clinical) skills gaps caused by staff rotations (this is really a restatement of the initial *Theory of Change* but emphasising the importance of continuity and repeat training). Further engagement with senior managers was pursued to improve accountability, build relationships between staff cadres improving the empowerment of midwives and responsiveness of doctors. The behavioural science model may characterise this as an individual motivation 'deficit.' At this stage in the process we tried to combine our earlier interventions targeted at individuals with a firmer focus on advocacy and policy implementation processes. This included more active engagement with high-level stakeholders and managers to remove barriers to the escalation process, reduce the potential for corruption to influence patient prioritisation and ensure that doctors are accountable and accessible.

**Outcome**: This proved to be a total failure: improving the presence and responsiveness of doctors has proven to be fundamentally resistant to change in spite of managerial interventions. Corruption continues to disrupt processes and resist change. Even the highest-level managers openly admitted that they lacked the power to challenge organised syndicates, the behaviour of senior doctors and corruption dynamics.

**Review and Theory Development**: At this point the search for relevant research and explanatory theories fans out beyond the initial 'simple' intervention spanning multiple disciplines to generate new and highly complex knowledge combinations; clinical knowledge declines in significance as theories of corruption, human resource management and knowledge transfer take on a new significance. The relevance and value of systematic review declines as the search for more composite and complex theories capable of understanding wider systemic and structural dynamics becomes essential to future interventions. Fundamentally, acknowledgement of the complexities of researcher/volunteer positionality and the very limited scope for foreigner engagement in anti-corruption interventions highlights the resilience (functionality) of existing systems and the limited scope for impact from external professional volunteering and Health Partnership intervention.

This case study has shown how the implementation of something as apparently simple as triage with the potential to significantly reduce maternal and neonatal mortality (and the need for emergency intervention) whilst also substantially reducing the costs of public services has proved impossible to implement.

Grounded local knowledge achieved through ongoing ethnographic methods has enabled us to begin to understand the importance of tacit knowledge and the barriers to change. Interventions focused on individual capabilities or opportunities and individual behaviour change will not achieve systems change in public health facilities in Uganda. The powerful impact of subversive (tacit) knowledge and vested interests render the current system fully functional for the status quo. In this environment, those health workers and managers (and there are many) who genuinely hope and strive for systems change inevitably find it impossible to imagine a new reality and engage in action-planning to achieve that. And, sadly, the system will close ranks on those individuals who risk putting their heads above the parapet. Table 5.1 summarises the processes outlined before and the emphasis on deficits at each stage.

## CASE STUDY 2: MANAGING OBSTETRIC EMERGENCIES

The majority of UK/Ugandan Health Partnerships focus on hospital–hospital relationships.[8] And most are headed up by senior clinicians, mainly doctors (Ackers and Porter 2011). Volunteer clinical trainees are also usually keen to be placed in large, congested, hospitals where high patient volumes and clinical complexity meet both altruistic and clinical exposure needs (Tate 2016).[9] This, coupled with the policy emphasis and associated metrics (embedded in the Millennium Development Goals) on maternal mortality, encourages an emphasis on those facilities where the majority of recorded deaths take place.

**Table 5.1**   Summary of triage (a 'complex intervention')

| Problem definition | Theory of change | Unit of change | Intervention type | Knowledge type | Methodological approach | 'Facts'/metrics |
|---|---|---|---|---|---|---|
| 1 Skills deficit | Co-production of protocols coupled with co-delivered CMEs will improve patient outcomes | Individual 'capability' | Simple | Knowledge deficit/functional Explicit/clinical/imported | Enumeration numerical test results | Empiricism |
| 2 Physical resource deficits | Providing resource (infrastructural improvements) will support implementation of new knowledge | Individual 'opportunity' | Complex | Explicit/technical | As above Audit | |
| 3 Human resource Deficits | Improving human resource management and accountability will enhance implementation | Individual 'opportunity' | Complex | Knowledge deficit/ functional tacit | Enumeration (staffing levels) | |
| 4 Power deficits | Implementation of co-produced knowledge impeded by systemic resistance/positionality | Organisational/ systemic intentionality' | High complex | Knowledge combinations tacit/ localised/embedded functional/ subversive | Ethnographic/ qualitative focus on process and system | Understanding Why? |

The SVP benchmarking process collated facility-held data on maternal mortality. Table 5.2 lists the main 'causes' of maternal deaths in Mulago National Referral Hospital in the 12 months from January 2012 to December 2012:

The data presented here should not be regarded as 'facts.' Certainly each maternal death recorded here is a sad fact but the process of establishing (single factor) causation is highly problematic. Significant pressure fuelled by SVP volunteers has encouraged a process of maternal mortality review, but compliance across the HUB remains patchy. As such, all facility-generated data must be regarded as a social construction.[10] Nevertheless, it serves one of the most important functions of quantitative data: it indicates trends and raises critical questions. During the early months of the LMP project (and very much playing the role of handmaiden to the obstetrician lead) we took it at face value that these were the causes of maternal deaths rather than the final 'hit' on the protracted 'road to death' (Filippi et al. 2005).

Faced with the alarming volume of maternal and neonatal deaths occurring in these referral facilities and the earlier 'evidence' on causation, it may come as no surprise that the overwhelming initial response was to advocate the introduction of (imported/amended) protocols and

**Table 5.2** Causes and frequencies of maternal deaths in Mulago (Jan-12 to Dec-12)

| Causes of death | Number of instances in 2012 |
| --- | --- |
| Abortion | 26 |
| Eclampsia | 22 |
| Post-partum haemorrhage (PPH) | 17 |
| Anaemia | 10 |
| Ruptured uterus | 11 |
| HIV-related | 21 |
| Respiratory distress | 2 |
| Cardiac arrest on table | 2 |
| Puerperal sepsis | 33 |
| Malaria in pregnancy | 8 |
| Tetanus | 0 |
| Ruptured ectopic | 4 |
| Dead on arrival | 1 |
| Total | **157** |

Source: McKay and Ackers 2013.

associated CME-style short-course training packaged under the generic title of 'Emergency Obstetric and Neonatal Care (EmONC)'. This was certainly our experience during our early involvement with the Liverpool-Mulago Partnership and, subsequently, in the Ugandan Maternal and Newborn Hub. And, in the first instance, as non-clinicians, we lacked the experiential knowledge and confidence to challenge the dominant medical paradigm. Indeed, in our report on Emergency Obstetric Skills Training conducted by SVP volunteers, we describe the intervention as an 'intensive two-day course designed to address the *main causes of maternal mortality* in resource poor settings in a systematic fashion' (Tate 2014). Several years and experience later we would question this 'diagnosis'.

The identification of the 'problem' at this stage in our learning was twofold: first, that many women are dying from (emergency) conditions that are preventable if staff had the right skills (to treat emergences). And, second, that Uganda lacks human resource capacity (clinicians do not possess the appropriate level of skill). Once again, this is immediately (evidently) apparent on the wards which are manned mainly by intern (junior) doctors.

**Initial Theory of Change**: The engagement of UK clinical volunteers alongside Ugandan counterparts in the adaptation of established 'Green Top Guidelines'[11] from the UK and associated (CME) training will reduce maternal and neonatal mortality.

### Intervention: Skills Deficits (Capabilities)

The intervention could be described as relatively simple[12] involving the transmission of explicit clinical skills. These included training in the value of observations and early warning scores (Case Study 1) and management of conditions such as eclampsia, haemorrhage and sepsis. As in Case Study 1, following the requirements of our funding body (THET), the immediate evaluation involved counting the volume of participants and simple before-and-after testing of skills acquisition (during the 2-day period). Combined with feedback forms, these instruments indicated a very marked improvement in skills and a strong expressed intentionality on the part of participants to utilise them.

In many interventions, this is where evaluation ends and training teams then 'fly-home.' Whilst pre- and post-testing measures typically indicate a high level of immediate impact, attempting to assess/project any causal (attributable) impact on mortality rates, etc., is ambitious and highly unlikely to succeed. Ethnographic observational methods combined with interviews indicated the application of some of the skills acquired amongst some of the trainees for a limited period of time and when in co-present relationships with volunteers. In practice, the ripples of good practice extending from these forms of training soon disappear.

*Outcomes*

Sadly, our research indicates that, although skills such as these can never be entirely wasted in terms of individual learning and potential; the investment in short CME-style interventions does not deliver the kinds of behaviour change capable of impacting public health systems in an effective, sustainable and efficient manner. Staff rotations make it especially difficult to monitor the skills use of those individuals whose skills gain is highest (junior doctors, interns and students). Whilst methods could have been developed to track individual journeys and attempt to assess skills use, the focus of the project on highly contextualised specific public facilities within the HUB discouraged this approach. Whilst we could have expended research resource to track individuals, we also felt quite strongly that implementation depends on achieving a level of critical mass capable of influencing cultural change within organisations supported by managerial buy-in.

Furthermore, many more established staff – and especially doctors – are not present on public wards with any degree of regularity to enable skills utilisation to take place (or be observed). And, many clinicians who are motivated to engage in training do so to facilitate career moves out of clinical work altogether, into the private sector (internal brain drain) or to clinical work in other countries (external brain drain). This proved to be the case with many of the clinicians who came to the UK supported by British Commonwealth Fellowships. Whilst the SVP objectives in bringing people to the UK were initially to enhance capabilities through training, the majority of fellows have used the credentials gained and networks established to exit clinical work in Uganda. In many cases they gained a new appetite for and confidence in international travel, immediately moving onto other courses in Sweden, Australia and Kenya (among others). Others have established their own NGOs or private training enterprises and become trainers themselves in Uganda, positioning themselves to harvest international NGO funding for CMEs. Others have sought direct employment in the private or NGO sector. Certainly the individual motivation in many cases is to use this experience to exit or reduce reliance on public sector clinical work.

When we assess data on human resources in Ugandan facilities, it is immediately apparent that the staff who are visibly present to professional volunteers (and form the basis of the presumption of a major skills shortage) represent the most junior of cadres (intern doctors and students). Large volumes of more experienced and highly trained staff, many of whom have had remarkable opportunities for international training, are simply not present on the wards to implement skills.

*Training Protocols in CMEs*

In the course of the SVP project, we were made aware of serious problems arising from varieties of foreign organisations coming into Uganda and training to their own national protocols/guidelines. This was resisted by local stakeholders who felt that they had perfectly sound guidelines endorsed by their own professional organisations and that using different systems confused staff and undermined efficacy. Attempts by the SVP to encourage multi-disciplinary and international collaboration, although welcomed, failed to encourage the necessary cooperation required (even within the UK).

The problems associated with selecting appropriate guidelines and protocols extend beyond this concern with imposing imported national systems. One might argue (as we did at one point) that internationally agreed protocols would overcome this tension. Our experience of working with WHO guidelines in our current Hand Hygiene Project[13] identifies further sources of complexity. In this case, Ugandan infection control specialists accustomed to training according to WHO 'African Partners for Patient Safety' (APPS) protocols[14] are also experiencing major implementation gaps. The problem arises when training ignores local contexts and assumes the existence of critical 'opportunities'. In our recent work, this included an assumption manifest in MOH guidelines (Fig. 5.1) that all facilities have running water, hand soap and single-use hand towels (or paper towels):

Such a situation would be unique in Ugandan public health facilities. Indeed, when we sent our project manager to visit the trainer's own facility, she advised us that recently they had no water due to the fact that bills had not been paid. On this occasion the staff and patients launched a protest, which forced authorities to restore water to the facility. On the basis of this lesson we then proposed that our own training in Fort Portal would be targeted very specifically to local conditions and embrace

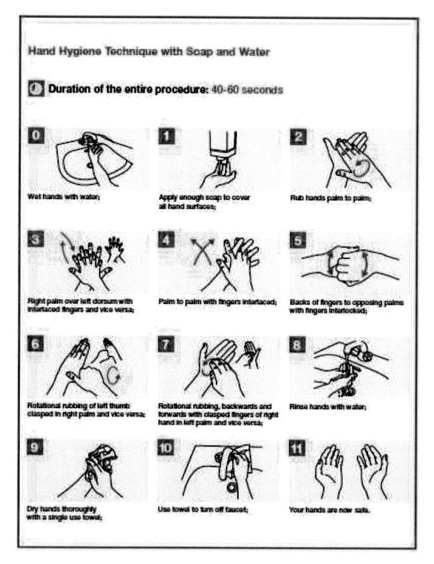

**Fig. 5.1** Ministry of Health guidance on Hand Hygiene (2014) (*Source*: Ugandan national infection prevention and control guidelines (MOH 2013))

an element of empowerment of local health workers and patients. Training Ugandan health workers using the APPS tools without careful attention to local conditions achieves nothing in practice and may even contribute to low morale.

This emphasises the importance of the 'opportunity' dimension of behaviour change. Certainly in the case of hand hygiene, we would argue that most health workers understand the need to wash their hands both for their own protection and that of their patients. But faced with the lack of running water, soap and single-use towels, they find it impossible to see the benefits of training and imagine the reality of improved patient safety.

The SVP Benchmarking data underlined the importance of context to behaviour and outcomes. In Mulago hospital, between January 2011 and October 2012, only one maternal death was recorded on the private ward compared to 183 on the public ward. The same staff, with the same training, are responsible for both groups of patients. Figures for the same time period evidence marked differences in C-section rates for the private and public ward.

C-section rates on the private ward are around double those on the public ward. Ongoing engagement with colleagues in the hospital made us aware of the 'policy' that all c-sections on the private ward should be undertaken by obstetric specialists and must be prioritised. These doctors receive 'top-up' pro rata payments for such procedures that dwarf monthly salaries. Given this information the need for EmONC training becomes less obvious.

### Intervention: Physical Resource Deficits (Opportunities)

As with Case Study 1 a logical complementary measure responding to claims on the part of healthcare workers that they lack basic physical resources to support emergency obstetric interventions was to provide equipment, infrastructure and consumables – the 'opportunities' enabling them to utilise their skills. And, the problems associated with resource management in Ugandan public health facilities underline the legitimacy of this claim. Few, if any, operating theatres in Health Centre IVs are fully functional and available for use.[15]

It is with this in mind that the SVP shifted its emphasis mid-project (and following requests by Ugandan stakeholders) away from large referral hospitals to address the efficacy of referral systems. This shift was also informed by evidence on the ground of the failure of CME interventions in congested hospitals to effect any perceptible systems change and further review of the research on maternal delays. These alternative conceptualisations of the causes of maternal deaths involving more longitudinal and holistic analyses and multi-disciplinary insights encouraged us to reconsider the data on the stated causes of maternal deaths (Table 5.2). Informed by research on the 'three delays' (Kaye et al. 2011; Pacagnella et al. 2012; Thaddeus and Maine 1990; Thorsen et al. 2012; Tuncalp et al. 2012) and our own research on the ground, our focus then became one of reducing delays in order to avoid preventable problems turning into obstetric emergencies (or deaths).

One of the sites in which this intervention took place was Kisenyi Health Centre IV, which refers patients into Mulago Hospital. At the time of intervention, this purpose-built facility with a full remunerated staffing complement had not been available to delivering mothers since opening 7 years previously.

Our revised *Theory of Change* at this point indicated a focus on restoring functionality to Health Centre IV facilities in order to increase deliveries, thereby reducing congestion in referral facilities and complications arising from maternal delays.

*Intervention*
The initial intervention (building on previous experience in two other facilities) involved an intense 1-week multi-disciplinary problem-solving exercise. In practice, most of the infrastructure, consumables and staff were present but small 'snagging' problems such as the lack of a sink in the delivery suite, the lack of drainage to wash floors and some basic equipment repair work and a lack of leadership had blocked progress. Within one week the first baby was delivered and, with new local leadership, the facility swung into action.

**Outcome**: Within 1 year, and following a series of very minor infrastructural and equipment interventions (costing the charity less than £1000 in total) the facility achieved a sustained average monthly delivery rate of over 800 (Ackers 2016). Every mother delivered in Kisenyi is one less mother delivering in Mulago. From that perspective, the impact on congestion and delays is tangible but not directly measureable/attributable[16] as many other factors will intervene to shape admissions (such as the closing of another major referral Health Centre at that time and a significant outbreak of typhoid).

Despite these successes in building Kisenyi into a fully functioning midwifery-led unit, the operating theatre remained under-utilised.

Improving functionality and providing associated training (including EmONC) supported by volunteer mentoring failed to reduce referrals for c-sections, which remained high, resulting in preventable deaths (Ackers 2016). At this stage, we could have significantly reduced referrals if we had allowed SVP volunteers to operate on patients in the absence of local doctors. We did not allow this breach of the co-presence principle. Chapter 2 reported on the audit conducted by the then SVP volunteer revealing key factors participating referrals (Fig. 5.2).

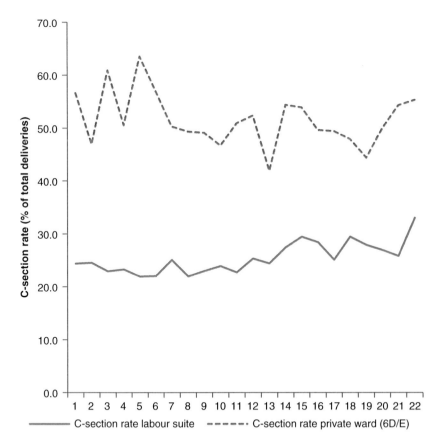

Fig. 5.2 Caesarean section rates on the private and public wards, Mulago Hospital (*Source*: McKay and Ackers 2013: 23)

These included supplies of blood, oxygen and power and the presence of doctors. Each of these components, whilst apparently 'simple', is in practice a can of worms. The availability of blood is itself a composite problem reflecting power supply (electricity); the adequacy and efficacy of the blood donation system, elements of corruption and also transportation. Power is also far more complex than meets the eye; shortages may reflect a failure to pay bills (and disappearance of relevant funds), (political) power play and funding shortages related to the purchase of fuel for back-up generators (a common problem in Uganda[17]) and the inflated costs of solar power in low-resource settings. On occasions any of these elements may be used and manipulated as excuses for inaction. However, as we have seen, the most common factor precipitating unnecessary referrals concerns physician presence.

Rather than go into detail about any of the aforementioned, we have decided to focus here on a more clinical follow-on intervention; namely, the institution of elective c-sections. Attempts to institute elective c-section lists have been repeatedly made by SVP volunteers across all HUB facilities. As one volunteer explains in her monthly report:

> It would help facilities if there was a regular elective day/s for cases that need a caesarean section to prevent mothers having to await labour and all its inherent risks when there are likely time delays in access to theatre. This would possibly reduce transfers, emergency sections and increased mortality/morbidity.

The institution of elective c-sections would further reduce maternal delays and the need for emergency/crisis intervention.

### Intervention: Implementing Elective (planned) Caesarean Sections

The overwhelming majority of caesarean sections in Uganda are undertaken as emergencies allowing complications to develop, delays to lengthen, outcomes to worsen and cost to escalate. A recent audit in Mulago Hospital (Acen 2015) found that of 200 C-sections undertaken in September to November 2014, 184 (92 %) were emergency sections. Introducing an electives c-section list in Health Centre IV Facilities would build on the success of SVP intervention to ensure more timely intervention, reducing complications and unnecessary and time-consuming referrals. On the face of it, this is a very simple intervention requiring training/mentoring in the clinical indications for c-section coupled with a staff rota and booking system.

*Intervention: Skills Deficits*
Most of the short courses in emergency obstetric care discussed in Chapter 3 include the discussion of indications and guidelines for elective sections. And this training has been embedded in the SVP through further short-course skills drills, ongoing mentoring and audit work to support implementation on the ground.

### Intervention: Resource Deficits (Stationary and Records Books)

A desk-book was made available to enable staff to book women for elective procedures.

*Outcome: Sporadic Minimal Improvement*
The provision of training, protocol development and mentoring coupled with the institution of an (unchallenged) booking system failed to improve c-section rates. This failure is in large part due to the persistent resistance of local doctors (and at times anaesthetic assistants) to be present and for local midwives to book patients (anticipating the former and resorting to the cultural 'if in doubt refer' logic). At this point the intervention develops a level of complexity implying engagement with highly sensitive power dynamics and generating problems of positionality both within the Ugandan human resource management system and in the relationships that 'outsiders' have with local staff and managers.

Figure 5.2 indicated that the presence of doctors was a major factor contributing to over 53 % of referrals. IF we discount referrals made at night over a quarter of referrals made during normal daytime working hours cite the lack of medical presence as a key reason (Fig. 5.3).

At this point, the level of complexity involved coupled with the difficulties that Health Partnerships and volunteers face as 'outsiders' with no real power to influence policy makers we attempted to offer moral support to brave local managers keen to incentivise and enforce accountability in human resource management systems. The in-charge midwife made considerable efforts to encourage doctors to be present and to expose those who were not present during their allocated working hours. And the City authorities (KCCA) increased doctors' pay (quite considerably) in Health Centre IV facilities and considered the potential of installing an electronic

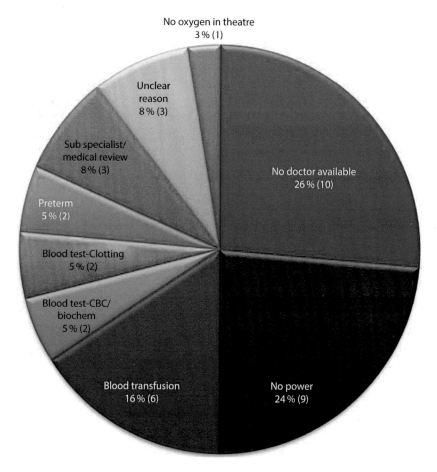

**Fig. 5.3**  Reasons for referrals between the hours of 08:00 and 17:00 Kisenyi Health Centre (*Source*: Ackers 2016 [*CBC*: Complete Blood Count])

system to record staff presence. In practice, this resulted in short-lived and minimal behaviour change and significant resistance to change among all doctors.

Somewhat surprisingly, some months later, continued facility benchmarking identified a sudden marked increase in elective c-section rates. Our first inclination was to celebrate the apparent success of ongoing interventions and regret our impatience. Our presence on the ground, however, and localised knowledge raised immediate concerns about this sudden shift. We were aware that one doctor was making a concerted effort to improve practice. However, we became suspicious that other 'entrepreneurial' practices were emerging as local doctors began to use the improved premises for private (fee-paying) elective c-sections. SVP volunteers are unable to 'prove' this situation empirically, given the subversive quality of corruption and the risks involved in openly asking questions – but they expressed concern when 'surprise' elective sections were observed to take priority over emergency cases. This is not the first time that investments made by our programme in improving infrastructure have stimulated an increase in private cases. Rather than indicating a problem caused by skills or knowledge deficits, we would conclude that our interventions have been manipulated through the use of highly entrepreneurial subversive local knowledge. summarises the processes outlined in the Case Studies:

The aforementioned case studies do not reflect the total (zero-sum) failure of interventions; capability-enhancing training combined with a focus on improving the opportunities for skills utilisation are necessary but insufficient constituents of change. Change can be seen to occur in terms of individual skills enhancement and, during volunteer co-presence, some partial skills utilisation and adherence to protocols. But these are key components in far more complex interventions. Understanding why these interventions, which typify the overwhelming majority of Health Partnership-style initiatives internationally, fail to translate into sustainable systems change is essential if we are to avoid wasting public money and undermining health systems.

## THE KNOWLEDGE DEFICIT MODEL

Why is it, given the lack of tangible evidence that AID, in any of its guises, works that funding continues to grow exponentially and continue to fund interventions that either do not work or generate damaging externality effects? And why, given the clear failure of existing evaluation metrics to capture the processes responsible for impact failure, is the solution seen as one of honing metrics? Public and political concern at the lack of impact of huge volumes of public funding has led to an increasing obsession with metrics and quantitative outcome measures.

The UK Department for International Development's 'logframe' methodology has had a major 'structuring impact' generating a common template for the evaluation of international development interventions. This formulaic approach has led to the emergence of a new (and highly confusing) conceptual vocabulary requiring projects to report, in a 'theory of change' approach on 'activities', 'inputs', 'outcomes' and 'outputs'. The THET, almost entirely reliant on DFID funding, has necessarily had to import this approach and apply it to all Health Partnership work. Sadly, this has forced a situation in which the 'tail has begun to wag the dog' as the clamour for funds begins to shape interventions around the demands of the funding bodies and their evaluation metrics rather than perceived needs or a grounded understanding of what works or does not. And this has a major impact on the use of evaluation resource; so great is the need to count 'outcomes' that there is little time to try to understand and make sense of failure. And failure is and has been the dominant outcome of development interventions for many decades.

The Lancet Commission's 'Global Surgery' report opens with the statement: 'Remarkable gains have been made in global health in the past 25 years' (Meara, J.G. et al 2015: 569) but provides no evidence to substantiate this claim. It goes on to present a very holistic and comprehensive case for multi-professional interventions informed by the three delays model and focused on 'broad-based health-systems solutions' (p. 570). The concluding section argues that 'research, monitoring and assessment play a crucial part in the future of global surgery' together with a 'commitment to better understand the problems and solutions' (p. 616). We would agree wholeheartedly with this prognosis. Having said that, we firmly believe that attributing this to the 'complete absence of globally accepted surgical metrics' entirely misses the point.

A recent report on International Development Funding by the UK Government's Public Accounts Committee found that, despite the trebling of public funding for humanitarian crises, 'the Department for International Development did not have a full understanding of where its money went' (House of Commons Report 2016). DFID defended its record arguing that it had a system which enabled it to 'aggregate the success of each intervention into a score which it can track month by month across interventions' (p. 10). However, it failed to report its portfolio score. What we are doing here is attempting to measure the measurable (as information or 'data') rather than the meaningful (as knowledge):

> Simplistically conceptualising knowledge as information makes its valuation and trade measurable but loses most of the originality of the empirical phenomenon. By contrast when scholars conceptualise knowledge as complex capabilities embodied in people and organisations, it no longer fits into the concept of an economic good that can be valued, traded, and accumulated, and its exact measurement becomes an impossibility. (Gluckler et al. 2013: 6)

These reports underline the fact that we know so little about the effectiveness of AID and that the solution to this problem is seen to lie in the production of ever-more quantitative metrics. No attempts are made to question the underlying epistemological biases of this logic or, put more simply, the fact that metrics have never worked and never will capture the 'problems and solutions' facing health systems in LMICs (or indeed the UK).

Fundamentally, we are suffering from a form of myopia generated by the domination of medical science perspectives or knowledge paradigms which determine the diagnoses, the interventions and epistemological approaches to evaluation. The quest for statistical outcomes (ideally gained through the gold standard of randomised controlled trials) underpinned by the narrowing blinkers of systematic review restricts our ability to understand social processes. There is also a tendency within this paradigm to pathologise or patronise individuals whilst failing to understand the impact of structural constraints. Despite growing recognition of the importance of context, this is often in the form of lip service at best acknowledging it as a cluster of variables that we don't understand (as external 'noise') or, at worst, rather than understanding and capturing its iterative quality, trying to insulate our interventions from it through vain or inappropriate attempts to control it. Trying to cleanse data through what feminist researchers have called a 'sanitisation process' (Harding 1987, 1991) will not generate cleaner facts. It will take us further away from the truth as the cleansing process strips data of its real value: of understanding the social processes that shape phenomenon. It may be that what we are swilling away in the effluent is that which is of greatest value.

This narrow conceptualisation of knowledge not only affects the approach to evaluation, but it also reproduces a partial understanding of knowledge mobilisation as an activity. The emphasis on explicit clinical skills and neglect of tacit knowledge leads to the identification of a 'knowledge deficit' encouraging uni-directional flows (from the host to the LMIC or from doctors to midwives). We are not adding skills to context (as the COM-B model implies): context lies at the heart of complex fluid and, oftentimes confounding knowledge combinations. Or, as McCormack puts it: 'nothing exists and can be understood in isolation from its context' (2015: 3009).

On the basis of our research and learning, we would argue that far from a skills deficit we are in a situation of knowledge saturation; clinical skills/ information are not the primary problem and using clinical 'experts' as conduits for yet more skills-forcing interventions is neither efficient nor effective. To the contrary, it is both arrogant and wasteful. This arrogance does not derive solely (although this certainly does contribute) to the imposition of 'expert information' from the global North: from well-meaning but narrow thinking foreign clinical experts and 'donors'. It is the consequence of a failure to see the bigger picture – of narrowing disciplinary knowledge paradigms. Although the lack of patient management is recognised as an issue by all UK clinicians working in Uganda: it was a visiting Ugandan obstetrician who proposed the initiative to introduce the African Maternal Early Warning Score (AMEWS) into Mulago Hospital. Enthralled by its apparent success in the UK (visiting foreigners are often not exposed to or fail to see the fundamental weaknesses of UK systems) she quite understandably attempted a 'policy transfer' approach: she 'saw' a clinical solution to a clinical problem and tried to transfer it. And as a project we sought to support her in this without comprehending the localised knowledge that would ultimately render it unsuccessful.

Knowledge can be both enabling and disabling; it is not only a deficit of skills/knowledge that hampers progress; narrow siloed knowledge (focused on harvesting facts) can limit our ability to see the social world and the truth that lies behind interventions. Resistance to change may be fuelled by knowledge and often quite entrepreneurial tacit localised knowledge. From an individual perspective – how to make ends meet and sustain your family – or, from a systems perspective – how to organise and funnel the rewards from systemic forms of corruption – requires a level of localised tacit knowledge and rational/entrepreneurial decision making that foreign volunteers may fail to 'see'.

The overall conclusion of this book, based on intense multi-method action-oriented research over a period of 8 years, is that international development initiatives in the form of Health Partnerships and through the mechanism of professional voluntarism (staff exchanges) are failing to bring about significant sustainable systems change in the Ugandan public health sector. Having said that, we believe that Health Partnership activity has the potential to mitigate the forms of systems damage associated with AID. More importantly, we believe it has the capacity to form the basis of evidence-based incremental systems change. Achieving this will require a much more structured approach to professional volunteer deployment based on principles of negotiated conditionality. Whilst we emphasise the importance of understanding the benefits and humility of increment-alism in policy change, from an epistemological perspective we need a paradigm shift.

If we reflect on the three scenarios presented in Chapter 1, we can conclude that the risks associated with Scenario 3 (negative impact through collateral damage) remain very high and most AID activity falls into this category. In terms of long-term sustainability, most of what we have achieved through the SVP would fall under Scenario 2 (neutral long-term impact but with minimal externality effects). More optimistically, and informed by the iterative learning we have experi-enced ourselves as researchers and project managers, we believe that Scenario 1 is achievable (partial improvement with minimal collateral damage).

The book opened and is peppered with firmly expressed concerns about the externality effects of AID focused on gap filling and service delivery. We have talked a lot about collateral damage, the unintended conse-quences of well-intentioned interventions and the critical importance of co-presence. When interventions, such as the SVP and the Health Partnership Scheme more generally, are based on sound conditionality principles, externality effects may be positive. Certainly the co-presence principle supports the active clinical engagement of professional volun-teers. In this process, the collateral benefits of systems focused interven-tion are enormous. We have no doubt and are reminded on a daily basis of the impacts of our work and of professional volunteers in particular on patient services and individual patients. SVP volunteers are saving the lives of mothers and babies in Uganda on a daily basis. Finally, the key bene-ficiaries of the SVP model are those patients who rely on public welfare to meet their healthcare needs, both in the immediate term (through the daily hands-on engagement of volunteers) and through longer-term sys-tems change.

The following section outlines some key elements of structure and conditionality that we have identified through our action-research journey. These concerns and the recommendations that accompany them may not be directly applicable or transportable to other LMIC or disciplinary contexts but when carefully contextualised and translated they could inform policy making and volunteer deployment.

## POLICY RECOMMENDATIONS

### 1. Corruption

Health Partnership interventions, as with all AID, generate vast opportunities for corruption. Opportunities for corruption are identified and exploited in every interaction we engage in from the use of disposable gloves to the donation of equipment. This is a highly entrepreneurial and innovative process which is very hard for 'outsiders' to see or to challenge. In this context, professional volunteers are often viewed as 'spies' and as such are open to forms of harassment. More commonly, they are unable to function effectively as clinicians and knowledge intermediaries.

*Recommendation 1: Whistle Blowing*
Health Partnerships and Volunteer Deployment Agencies need to work closely with their Ugandan partners on the ground and provide support mechanisms for volunteers to encourage them to recognise and report corruption. Health Partnerships are often loath to acknowledge or take action on corruption for fear of damaging relationships. This, in itself, damages relationships.

### 2. Labour Substitution

Our research indicates a significant potential for system damage when interventions are framed inappropriately to the context and when the context is itself misunderstood. Labour substitution is a huge risk. It undermines systems, distorts local labour markets and accentuates existing human resource management problems actively encouraging absenteeism and moonlighting (dual working). It is also profoundly arrogant. This 'style' of volunteering stems from traditional donor–recipient models and is particularly associated with missionary-style volunteering. The focus on 'helping' individual patients and creating parallel institutions for this purpose (mission hospitals etc.), whilst perfectly understandable, in the wider scheme of things undermines universal public health systems.

*Recommendation 2.1: Advocacy in Human Resource Management*
The efficacy of professional voluntarism will not improve unless key stakeholders in LMICs introduce and enforce accountability in human resource management systems. Measures must be put in place to ensure the timely payment of salaries and to discipline and/or dismiss staff members who fail to comply and present themselves for work. Unless local staff are present in the workplace, the opportunities for knowledge mobilisation and systems change are minimal. Specific attention needs to be paid to staff in leadership and senior positions, especially doctors. If leaders fail to present themselves for work in a timely manner, the lack of effective role modelling reinforces a culture of bad practice. Leadership is seriously lacking in most Ugandan health facilities. We do not believe this represents a need for training, however, but for improved accountability.

*Recommendation 2.2: Co-Presence*
All efforts should be taken to respect and embed the principle of co-presence when deploying professional volunteers. This should be interpreted as a key component of conditionality and where co-presence is not possible volunteers should be required to withdraw from that context. The only exception to this should be in carefully managed and documented emergency situations. The failure to respect co-presence by volunteer deploying organisations and individual volunteers undermines the position of those who are respecting the principle and generates resentment. Managing and operationalising co-presence requires the development of highly structured programmes for volunteer deployment with clear role descriptions and reporting mechanisms. 'Lone Ranger' and Missionary-style volunteering undermines these processes.

The enforcement of co-presence as a key dimension of accountability in human resource management systems requires high-level action at ministerial level and involving consortiums of international NGOs working in collaboration. This is the single most critical element of conditionality.

### 3. Equality and Ethical Standards in Volunteer Deployment

The THET has played a major role in supporting (and requiring) more structured, risk-assessed and ethical approaches to volunteer deployment. We believe that this has gone a long way to ensuring that the recruitment and deployment of professional volunteers complies with UK equality law and policy. However, we have witnessed behaviour on the part of UK-registered Charities operating in Uganda, particularly those involved in Mission Hospitals (affecting both Ugandan health workers and UK volunteers) which would seriously breach all equality rules in the UK. This includes overt discrimination on grounds of sexuality, gender, race, religious beliefs and breaches of the principles of the Working Time Directive and work–life balance.

*Recommendation 3: Equality and Charitable Status*
We have noted (earlier) our concern at the role that faith-based NGOs (charities) play in running parallel organisations independent of the Ugandan public health sector. As a general rule, we believe this process undermines the public system and creates opportunities to extend damaging forms of missionary-style colonialism. These exist in a 'bubble' with apparent immunity from both Ugandan and UK law and policy and attract religious fanatics. All UK charities operating in LMICs should be required to abide by both Ugandan and UK Employment, Charity and Equality Laws. Failure to comply should result in loss of charitable status.

### 4. The Commodification of Training

It is inappropriate and wasteful to pay people (per diems) to receive training. The payments attached to training have distorted the whole meaning of training and created a situation where people are training for the wrong reasons and the wrong people are consuming the opportunities on offer. The failure of LMICs and development organisations to develop a common policy on this generates tensions and a competitive environment, which further detracts from knowledge mobilisation objectives. AID organisations have commodified training, creating new opportunities for corruption and serial absenteeism especially among senior staff and 'leaders'.

*Recommendation 4: Per Diems*
The practice of providing per diems for training should be immediately stopped. We urge the Ugandan Ministry of Health and District Health Offices to create protocols to regulate these practices so that training interventions reach the people they are designed for and perverse incentives are extinguished. Providing essential assistance with transport and refreshments is less of a problem. Organising training events as close as possible to health workers' work place and, where possible, in the workplace reduces these costs (and risks) whilst also reducing the amount of time health workers are away from the wards.

## 5. Internal Brain Drain

Often overlooked, internal brain drain has a far greater impact on the human resource 'crisis' in LMICs than external brain drain (emigration). And development interventions create significant opportunities for this through the employment of staff in project management and other roles. This is a complex issue. What is clear from our research is that the clamour for 'project employment' is having a hugely distorting effect on national labour markets and career development strategies. The effect of this is to encourage an emphasis on non-clinical postgraduate qualifications (Masters in Business Administration or Public Health for example) as part of a planned exit from clinical work. This is often seen as the alternative to dual working (internal brain drain into the private sector whilst in full-time public employment), which blocks positions for early career health workers.

*Recommendation 5: Remunerating Staff in LMICs*
There is no simple solution to this complex ethical problem. We are, quite rightly, encouraged by funding bodies to employ local staff where possible and build capacity in leadership and management. However, we believe that local staff should receive a level of remuneration broadly parallel to what they would (or should) receive in their public roles. We have tried to identify the level of pay that delivers a 'living wage' as opposed to the (below) subsistence-level pay that health workers are receiving in Uganda. Ultimately the MOH needs to increase health worker pay quite significantly for all cadres and impose a level of accountability to ensure that those who are paid are present and work effectively.

We would propose that a doubling of health worker salaries could be achieved at no cost and with marked efficiencies by dismissing all those staff who fail to report for work. Once this level is achieved and staff members are paid on time, foreign organisations should remunerate at national rates. From a system perspective, it is irresponsible and unethical to remunerate health workers in Uganda at rates common in the UK or the USA.

### 6. Continuing Professional Development (or Continuing Medical Education)

Health Partnership interventions have focused on the provision of short courses aimed at health workers. Uganda lacks an active CPD programme in most professional areas and there is little evidence of active Professional Development Review Systems. In some areas such as bio-medical engineering they are entirely absent. This leaves a vacuum for foreign organisations. In isolation and without follow-up, one-off short courses do little to change professional behaviour; ongoing mentoring on the job increases the opportunities for health workers to gain confidence and skills; this is a necessary but insufficient condition for individual behaviour change.

*Recommendation 6.1: Professional Development Review*
CPD/CME training needs to be embedded within a comprehensive PDR process for health workers so that needs are identified by line managers and training is organised to meet those needs.

*Recommendation 6.2: Post-Training Mentoring Is Critical to Knowledge Mobilisation*
One-off formal CMEs are effective in transmitting information. Operational isation and application of that learning needs support on the job to build confidence and hone skills. Professional volunteers along with their peers have a potentially valuable role to play in this process. Notwithstanding the pressure on health workers, Uganda does have many experienced clinicians. It is important that these staff members are required to support volunteers in the training and mentoring process as part of their professional role (and not on a top-up fee basis). At the present time, there is very little evidence of supervision and mentoring on the part of experienced Ugandan clinicians and we should take care not to substitute or commodify these roles. Careful thought should be given to the value of taking staff away from their clinical

duties for one-off training if there are no mechanisms in place to support post-course co-working and mentoring.

## 7. Donations

Donations of equipment, consumables or cash distort relationships and generate misunderstandings, which pose problems for subsequent interventions and volunteer activities. Professional volunteers are often seen first and foremost as 'donors' or, more crudely but accurately, 'cash cows'. The SVP and its sister bio-medical engineering project have drawn attention to the serious problems associated with donated equipment, much of which lies unused or unusable creating problems for storage and infection control. It also means that managers often lack awareness of what equipment there is in their facilities. On a more mundane level, it is important to explain to prospective volunteers the importance of discussing donations and requests for cash support, etc., with the project managers.

*Recommendation 7: Donations Policies*
All organisations, both in the sending country and in the LMIC, should adopt a transparent and joined-up donations policy. However kind and generous the intentions, the act of donation can pollute relations and generate problems. Care should be taken whenever providing infrastructural support to public facilities. The provision of consumables and equipment generates dependency, encourages opportunities for corruption and is entirely unsustainable. Where support is provided, the objective should be to provide the very minimum of support to leverage local systems rather than substituting for them. We consider this to be an example of 'snagging' where a whole facility can be out of action because there is no sink, for example, but local staff exist to install the sink. When providing support the SVP and our sister bio-medical engineering project developed a firm policy on donations.[18]

## 8. Evaluation: Efficacy and Meaning

We have described the SVP project as a journey. This has been mainly a research journey. We embarked upon it with an extensive background in multi-methods, comparative, high-impact social research. Throughout this journey we have experienced a creative tension with the evaluation arm of the funding body and with other organisations and stakeholders in the global health field. This discomfort has generated active learning for us as researchers unfamiliar with the foundations of medical research, its dominance across health sciences and the quite similar metrics paradigm framing international development. Our concerns about the epistemological bias of these approaches and their inability to capture social context and process are well rehearsed in the book. But we have another concern about the efficacy of evaluation. The Health Partnership Scheme in common with so many other funders of global health has begun to conceptualise every actor in a funded project as a researcher. On one level we commend that and it resonates with our ethical commitment to co-researching. The problem is that researching such complex interventions requires a very high degree of research expertise and is hugely time-consuming. Partners in HP projects do not have the time or necessarily the expertise to undertake extensive literature reviews or policy analysis work; neither do they possess the skills to develop research plans and operationalise mixed-methods studies. And, they may well not have the experience, time or desire to engage in complex data analysis and writing up. Whilst all actors can become engaged in action-research projects and we have certainly viewed our Ugandan colleagues and professional volunteers as co-researchers, finally a considerable research expertise is required to design, manage and make sense of the data.

On that basis we would question the pressure put on all projects to conduct in-depth, expensive and time-consuming evaluation. Certainly attempts to aggregate core indicators across the diversity of projects will achieve nothing apart from churning out meaningless and potentially misleading statistics.

### Recommendation 8: Evaluation Policy

We would recommend that valuable resource expended on evaluation be used more wisely to conduct expert research on a sample of interventions managed by researchers with proven expertise. Many private consultancy organisations lack academic research training and experience and constitute an expensive and poor-quality 'offer'. The British Academy Report on the role of the Humanities and Social Sciences in Public Policy Making (Wilson 2008) expressed concern at the very high proportion of UK government department's research budgets that were being 'allocated to short-term projects to meet current political and administrative demands' arguing that the government was failing to leverage the academic research base. Identifying the demands of complex inter-departmental collaborations straddling the boundaries of departments, it argues that 'many challenges require a more sophisticated understanding of human behaviour' (Executive Summary p. 1). The report concurs with our recommendation that research funding should be focused more into support longitudinal peer-reviewed knowledge development.

## Knowledge for Change?

A common response when we present our research findings is to ask us why we carry on with the work when the outcomes are so bleak and depressing. We do not find the work depressing. Indeed, to the contrary, it has been quite liberating. We cannot begin to develop interventions that have the potential to bring about systems change unless we have the knowledge base to understand the context and the processes involved. Trying to understand another country and co-design complex interventions takes time; it also challenges our skills as researchers and activists. This book has been written at a particular juncture in this learning process. We will carry on learning but we feel that we have achieved a level of understanding (and knowledge base) now that can and should be shared with others to reframe interventions.

We have always enjoyed the company of our Ugandan colleagues. We do not regard ourselves as 'donors' or them as 'recipients': rather we regard each other as fellow professionals. And we would like to move away from the language of helping or volunteering to speak more collegially about international faculty. We know from previous research and common experience that international exposure tends to reinforce rather than challenge stereotypes. Researchers and volunteers new to the field will unwittingly been drawn into absorbing and echoing those stereotypes: of Ugandan health workers as poorly trained and under-skilled, lazy, demotivated, lacking respect for fellow humans and corrupt. And the landscape we 'see' may reinforce this perception. Some of the research we have encountered along the way, notably from behavioural science perspectives, has the unintentional tendency to add intellectual credibility to these stereotypes often essentialising human behaviour. The work of evolutionary economics has given us fresh insight and lifted us from the traps of individualism, enabling us to forge genuine human relationships with our Ugandan colleagues as fellow human beings. Finally, there is more that we share than that which distinguishes us: context is indeed everything.

# NOTES

1. Which, according to the *Oxford English Dictionary*, is 'a thing which is hoped for but is illusory or impossible to achieve'.
2. The term 'theory' when used in the context of a 'theory of change' either in health sciences research or, quite commonly, in international development evaluation has a much narrower and more specific meaning than 'theory' in social science. It may be easier to view it as a form of working hypothesis.
3. According to Wikipedia: '**Triage** is the process of determining the priority of patients' treatments based on the severity of their condition. This rations patient treatment efficiently when resources are insufficient for all to be treated immediately'.
4. Funded by THET as part of the Ugandan Maternal and New born HUB grant.
5. Various adaptations of UK Maternal Early Warning Scoring systems have been introduced throughout the HUB. In practice, it has proved impossible to encourage all HPs to adopt the same system. The MEWS is a form of patient management system designed to enable staff to identify the sick patient and respond accordingly.
6. It is important to point out that our subsequent decision, as part of the THET-funded bio-medical engineering project we are running in parallel to the SVP has engaged with the 'opportunities' dilemma by providing the technicians that we are training across the HUB with a toolkit. WE also provided high-quality tool boxes for the technicians to store their tools in. This has been a resounding success with very little evidence of losses or thefts over 2 years after the intervention. In this example, the technicians have been working as part of a close team or Community of Practice with close attention to personal ownership and accountability.
7. Land lines are rare and staff are usually expected to use their own air time for such calls.
8. We are using the example of EmONC here but the same conclusions apply to all similar forms of CME-style training that volunteers have been involved in including neonatal resuscitation courses, which rarely if ever translate into effective practice and safer anaesthesia programmes.
9. Volunteer motivations are discussed in detail in Chatwin et al. (2016).
10. Language is also a problem; the term 'abortion' is used in Uganda to refer to miscarriages. Many of these are in fact (illegal) abortions.
11. https://www.rcog.org.uk/en/guidelines-research-services/guidelines/?p=5.
12. In the sense that training in critical care was seen as the primary objective.
13. For details see www.knowlege4change.org.uk.
14. See http://www.who.int/patientsafety/implementation/apps/en/.

15. The Health Sector Strategic Plan (2010/2011–2014/2015) includes a target of 'increasing the functionality of the HC IVs from 5 % to 50 %' (p. 48).
16. There was a drop in admissions to Mulago for the first time since 2000 but we cannot claim attribution.
17. Wherever fuel is involved there are high risks of corruption and a lack of 'petty cash'.
18. The K4C Induction Pack advises students and volunteers about donations: www.knowledg4change.org.uk, p. 24.

# Annex 1 – The Sustainable Volunteering Project

## Background and Objectives

The Sustainable Volunteering Project (SVP) is managed by the Liverpool-Mulago Partnership (LMP) and was initially funded by the UK Department for International Development via the Tropical Health and Education Trust's Health Partnership Scheme. Financial support has also been received from the Royal College of Obstetricians and Gynaecologists (RCOG) and the Association of Anaesthetists of Great Britain and Ireland (AAGBI). The THET-funded project began in April 2012 and ran for a 3-year period, ending March 2015. The SVP continues and is now funded in association with our partner charity Knowledge for Change (www. knowlege4change.org.uk/).

The LMP had been placing professional volunteers in Kampala for over 4 years before applying for funding for the SVP. The SVP, however, marked a substantial increase in the scale and scope of this activity; widening the LMP's focus outside of Kampala to support other Health Partnerships involved within the Ugandan Maternal & Newborn Hub (UMNH) and also broadening the cadres of Health Professionals supported to include not only obstetricians but also paediatricians, anaesthetists, midwives, nurses and biomedical engineers. UMNH is a consortium of UK-Uganda Health Partnerships established by the LMP in 2011 and encompassing the LMP, the Basingstoke-Hoima Partnership for Health,

© The Author(s) 2017                                                                    151
H.L. Ackers, J. Ackers-Johnson, *Mobile Professional Voluntarism*
*and International Development*, DOI 10.1057/978-1-137-55833-6

the Gulu-Manchester Health Partnership, the PONT-Mbale Partnership, the Bristol-Mbarara Link, the Kisiizi-Chester Partnership, the Kisiizi-Reading Partnership and a partnership between Salford University, Mountains of the Moon University and the Kabarole Health District.

The professional volunteers complete placements of varying lengths (between 6 and 24 months) and engage in a variety of initiatives, training programmes and on-the-job mentoring schemes which aim to increase capacity and improve the skills of the health workers, both in Uganda and in the UK. The SVP's focus is on capacity building and systems change and its objectives are twofold:

1. To support evidence-based, holistic and sustainable systems change through improved knowledge transfer, translation and impact.
2. To promote a more effective, sustainable and mutually beneficial approach to international professional volunteering (as the key vector of change).

The SVP does not have a focus on service delivery or workforce substitution as this activity is not judged to be sustainable.

## LTV MANAGEMENT AND SUPPORT

### Recruitment

All SVP volunteers are recruited, selected and managed by the LMP (and more recently also K4C). The main organisations targeted during the initial LTV recruitment were the Royal Colleges of Obstetrics and Gynaecology, Anaesthetists, Nursing and Midwives. The Royal Colleges either circulated an advertisement by email or posted it on their websites. The advertisements were also circulated by UMNH members to their local deaneries and hospitals. This initial advertisement process was successful in raising sufficient interest from prospective LTVs; the key to the success being the LMP's ability to utilise the existing links and networks established over previous years. As the project matured, an increasing number of LTVs were recruited through word-of-mouth advertisement by previous SVP LTV's and during project dissemination events, national and international conferences and workshops. Examples of such events include the British Maternal and Fetal Medicine Society's 'Annual Conference' (2013), the AAGBI's

'World Anaesthesia Society Conference' (2013), the Global Women's Research Society Conference (2012) and the Development Studies Association's 'Annual Conference' (2013).

## Selection

Following an initial expression of interest, two processes are run simultaneously before a candidate can be recruited to the SVP. The first process involves prospective LTVs completing an application form and attending an interview (usually face to face) in order to ascertain, for example, whether a candidate would be suitable, when and why they wish to undertake a placement, what support they might require, what they hope to achieve and what skills they possess which would be of benefit to the health system in Uganda. Two references are required to objectively verify a candidate's suitability and identify any additional support they may require.

The second process involves circulating the candidates' details to UMNH partnerships to assess which of them would be interested in hosting the candidate should they be recruited to the SVP. This process was designed to align the supply of LTVs with demand on the ground in Uganda and the ability of the local UMNH partnerships to host them. An LTV is only recruited if both of the aforementioned selection processes yield positive results.

## Placement Logistics

The subsequent stage following an LTV's recruitment is their pre-placement induction. Each LTV is provided with a comprehensive induction pack containing useful information on UMNH placement locations, what to expect in Uganda, placement logistics and travel, insurance and emergency contact details, health and safety and advice on pensions and other personal finances. LTVs receive a 'Volunteer Agreement' to sign and return to LMP management, which outlines the LMP's organisational expectations, a code of conduct, a statement on co-presence, potential disciplinary procedures and a personalised role description. Volunteer agreements are drawn up in conjunction with the LTV, the relevant UMNH partner organisation and the in-country counterparts to maximise stakeholder involvement and ensure all parties remain informed and satisfied.

Each placement location/facility and all LTV accommodations was professionally risk assessed at the beginning of the SVP. This risk assessment is shared with LTVs in advance of their placement, advising them of the potential risks of placements in Uganda, how the risks can be mitigated and what to do in the case that the risk materialises. The LMP also purchased a bespoke and comprehensive travel and medical insurance policy at the beginning of the SVP to cover all LTVs, ensuring each of them had adequate and sufficient cover throughout their placements. Having one familiar and reliable insurance policy and emergency contact number for all LTVs is beneficial in terms of project management and reduces individual LTVs and organisational risk.

In addition to insurance, the LMP also arranges LTV flights, clinical registration, visa/work permit, accommodation, airport transfers and the majority of placement-related travel in line with the recommendations of the risk assessment. The risk and logistical burden put on LTVs is reduced by, for example, using safe and reliable drivers for travel, only selecting flights that arrive at suitable times and only using safe and risk-assessed accommodation. Controlling these processes centrally allows for better coordination and achieves some economies of scale in terms of the procurement.

### *Placement Support*

LTVs have access to a wide range of support during their placements. In terms of financial support, LTVs receive a monthly stipend to assist them in covering their costs at home and in Uganda. The stipend is paid directly into their bank account, with the initial payment being made on the date of their outbound flight and consecutive recurrent payments made at monthly intervals. The Tropical Health and Education Trust's Health Partnership Scheme is able to fund the employer and employee pension contributions of those LTVs previously employed by the UK NHS for the duration of their placements, marking a less direct yet potentially hugely beneficial provision of financial support for LTVs.

Each LTV is assigned a UK and a Ugandan mentor to provide clinical, mental and pastoral support and advice during their placement. Suitable mentors are selected by the LMP in collaboration with UMNH partners and in-country stakeholders, and usually come from the same disciplinary background as the LTV as well as having previous experience of working/volunteering in Uganda. Many of the UK mentors selected are themselves former SVP LTVs who have returned to the UK but are keen to retain links with the project. The mentors serve as a first point of contact for LTVs; however, frequent communication with LMP management is also encouraged in case any problems arise that the mentors cannot deal with. LTVs provide written reports to LMP management on a monthly basis so their health and well-being can be monitored.

SVP workshops are held every 6 months. All SVP LTVs and stakeholders are invited to attend along with other LTVs working on similar projects; for example, the 'Global Links' project run by the Royal College of Paediatrics and Children's Health. Each LTV conducts a short presentation detailing their placement activity, successes and any challenges faced. The events stimulate useful discussion and learning and enable the LTVs to build networks which provide platforms for effective peer-to-peer support, partnership and co-working.

### *Project Evaluation*

An extensive and comprehensive evaluation programme has been carried out for the duration of the SVP. Data are collected by LMP management and evaluation teams, PhD students and the LTVs themselves for evaluation purposes and includes the following:

- Pre-, mid- and post-placement interviews with LTVs
- LTV written monthly reports (containing qualitative and quantitative data)
- Interviews with Ugandan Health Facility management and staff
- Interviews with UMNH partnership coordinators
- Interviews with LTV mentors
- Recorded workshops and focus groups
- Site visits and observations made by the LMP evaluation team
- Logging of stakeholder email communication
- Reviews of new and existing literature relating to professional volunteering
- Publications and presentations conducted by the LTVs at conferences and other dissemination events

All data are collected, anonymised, coded and analysed using Nvivo software. The SVP has evolved and strengthened on an iterative basis since its beginning in April 2012, based on the outcomes of the project evaluation and the growing experience of the project managers.

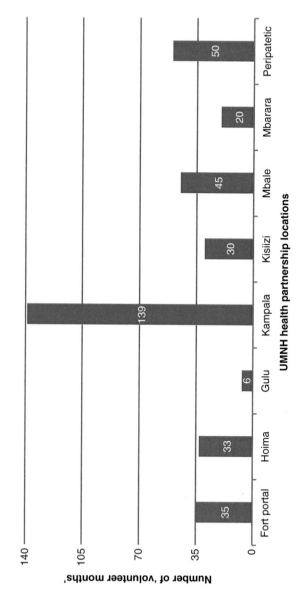

**Fig. A.1** Number of 'volunteer months' spent at each UMNH health partnership location

## LTV Deployment within the SVP

The SVP placed 44 professional volunteers across the UMNH partnership locations over the course of the initial 3-year period between April 2012 and March 2015, achieving a combined total of 358 'volunteer months'. The total number of volunteer months spent at each UMNH location is illustrated in Fig. A.1. The average (mean) placement duration across all disciplines was 8.1 months; however, the most common placement duration (modal average) was 6 months. The shortest placement duration was 1 month (the volunteer ended their 6 months' placement early) and the longest placement was 26 months.

The professional volunteers came from nine broad professional backgrounds; the highest number coming from Anaesthesiology (10) and the lowest number coming from General Practice (1) and Biomedical Engineering (1). Table A.1 details the number of volunteers deployed from each of the disciplinary backgrounds and the total number of volunteer placement months completed. Multidisciplinary team working was a key feature within the SVP and was believed to be the most effective way of achieving the desired outcomes of the project.

**Table A.1**   SVP volunteers by professional background

| Health professional disciplinary background | Number deployed during the SVP | Total combined number of volunteer months |
|---|---|---|
| Anaesthetists | 10 | 71 |
| Obstetricians | 9 | 60 |
| Midwives | 8 | 60 |
| Nurses | 6 | 48 |
| Foundation Year 2 doctors | 4 | 30 |
| Paediatricians | 3 | 33 |
| Social scientists | 2 | 24 |
| Biomedical engineers | 1 | 26 |
| General practitioners | 1 | 6 |
| **Total:** | **44** | **358** |

# References

Academy of Medical Royal Colleges. (2013). Academy statement on volunteering. Health Professional Volunteers and Global Health Development.

Acen, J. (2015). Satisfaction of post caesarean section mothers with pain management at Mulago national referral hospital. Unpublished Master's Thesis.

Ackers, H.L. (2013). From 'partial migrations' to mundane transnationalism: Socio-legal (re) conceptualisations of contemporary intra-EU migration. On-Line Journal on Free Movement of Workers within the EU. Issue 6. http://ec.europa.eu/social/main.jsp?catId=475&langId=en.

Ackers, H.L. (2014). The importance of volunteer/health worker relationships to project outcomes. SVP Policy Report at www.knowledge4change.org.uk.

Ackers, H.L. (2016). Project Report on Kisenyi Health Centre. Available at www.knowledge4change.org.uk/.

Ackers, H. L. (2015). Mobilities and knowledge transfer: Understanding the contribution of volunteer stays to North-South healthcare partnerships. *International Migration, 53*(1), 131–147.

Ackers, H.L., & Gill, B. (2008). *Moving people and knowledge: Scientific mobility in an enlarging Europe*. Northampton, MA: Edward Elgar.

Ackers, H.L., Gill, B.,Groves, K., & Oliver, E.A. (2006). Assessing the impact of enhanced salaries and stipends on postdoctoral and postgraduate positions. Research Councils UK. http://www.rcuk.ac.uk/RCUK-prod/assets/documents/skills/salariesstipends.pdf.

Ackers, H.L., & Porter, C.P. (2011). Evaluation of the NHS perspective of health links with developing countries. International Health Links Centre, Liverpool School of Tropical Medicine.

© The Author(s) 2017
H.L. Ackers, J. Ackers-Johnson, *Mobile Professional Voluntarism and International Development*, DOI 10.1057/978-1-137-55833-6

Ackers, H.L., & Ackers-Johnson, J. (2013). Understanding co-presence in the sustainable volunteering project. SVP Policy Report at www.knowledge4 change.org.uk.

Ackers, H.L., Lewis, E., & Ackers-Johnson, J. (2014). Identifying and mitigating risks in medical voluntarism – Promoting sustainable volunteering to support maternal and infant well-being in Uganda. *Journal of Medical Safety, International Association of Risk Management in Medicine*.

Ackers, H.L., Ackers-Johnson, J., Chatwin, J., & Tyler, N. (2016a). *Healthcare, frugal Innovation, and professional voluntarism: A cost-benefit analysis.* Palgrave.

Ackers, H.L., Ioannou, E., & Ackers-Johnson, J. (2016b). The impact of delays on maternal and neonatal outcomes in Ugandan public health facilities: The role of absenteeism. *Health Policy and Planning*, 1–10. doi: 10.1093/heapol/czw046.

Ahmed, A., Ackers-Johnson, J., and Ackers, H.L. (2016a). *The Ethics of Healthcare Education Placements in Low-Income Countries First Do Not Harm?* Palgrave.

Ahmed, A., Ackers-Johnson, J., Ackers, H.L., & Chatwin, J. (2016b). 'First do no Harm': Undergraduate learning and impacts during electives in low and middle income countries. New York: Palgrave.

Balikuddembe, M., Byamugisha, J., & Siekikubo, M. (2009). The Impact of decision-operation interval on pregnancy outcomes amongst mothers who undergo emergency caesarean sections at Mulago Hospital. Makerere University College of Health Sciences.

Barbard, C., Deakin, S., & Hobbs, R. (2001). Capabilities and rights: An emerging agenda for social policy? *Industrial Relations Journal, 32*(5), 464–479.

Bate, P. (2014). Context is everything. In *A selection of essays considering the role of context in successful quality improvement* (pp. 3–30). London: Health Foundation.

Benzies, K.M., Premji, S., Hayden, K.A., & Serrett, K. (2006). State-of-the-evidence reviews: Advantages and challenges of including grey literature. *Worldviews Evidence Based Nursing, 3*(2), 55–61.

Bolton, G. (2007). *AID and other dirty business.* London: Ebury Press.

Brocas, I., & Carillo, J.D. (Eds.). (2004). *The psychology of economic decisions,* Vol. II. Oxford: Oxford University Press.

Buchan, J. (2000). Health sector reform and human resources: Lessons from the United Kingdom. *Health Policy and Planning, 15*(3), 319–325.

Buchan, J. (2004). What difference does ("good") HRM make? *Human Resources for Health, 2*(6). http://www.human-resources-health.com/content/2/1/6.

Byrne-Davis, L., Byrne, G., Jackson, M., Abio, A., McCarthy, R., Slattery, H., Yuill, G., Stevens, A., Townsend, J., Armitage, C., Johnston, M., & Hart, J. (2016). Understanding implementation of maternal acute illness management education by measuring capability, opportunity and motivation: A mixed methods study in a low income country. *Journal of Nursing Education and Practice, 6*(3), 59–70.

Cane, J., O'Connor, D., & Michie, S. (2012). Validation of the theoretical domains framework for use in behaviour change and implementation research. *Implementation Science, 7*(37). http://www.implementationscience.com/con tent/7/1/37.

Canibano-Sanchez, C., Muñoz, P.F., & Encinar-del-Pozo, M. (2006). Evolving capabilities and innovative intentionality: Some reflections of the role of intention within innovation processes. *Innovation: Management, Policy and Practice, 8*, 310–321.

Chatwin, J., Ackers, H.L., Ackers-Johnson, J., & Ahmed, A. (2016). *Transformational learning? The value of international placements for professional health workers and their employers*. New York: Palgrave.

Chen, L., Evans, T., Boufford, J.I., Brown, H., Chowdhury, M., Cueto, M., Dare, L., Dussault, G., & Elzinga, G. (2004). Human resources for health: Overcoming the crisis. *The Lancet, 364*, 1984–1990.

Chopra, M., Munro, S., Lavis, J., Vist, G., & Bennett, S. (2008). Effects of policy options for human resources for health: An analysis of systematic reviews. *The Lancet, 371*, 668–674.

Clifton, J. (2007). *Global migration patterns and job creation*. Washington, DC: Gallup Poll. http://www.gallup.com/businessjournal/101680/global-migra tion-patterns-job-creation.aspx.

Cope, J. (2003). Entrepreneurial learning and critical reflection. *Management Learning, 34*(4), 429–450.

Cope, J. (2011). Entrepreneurial learning from failure: An interpretive phenomenological analysis. *Journal of Business Venturing, 26*, 604–623.

Cox, S. (2015, May 21) Where is Nepal aid money going? BBC Radio 4's 'The Report'.

CRD (NHS Centre for Reviews and Dissemination). (2001). *Undertaking systematic reviews of research on effectiveness: CRD's guidance for those carrying out or commissioning reviews (2nd ed)*. York: CRD. Report number 4.

Crisp, N. (2007). *Global health partnerships. The UK contribution to health in developing countries*.

Crisp, N. (2010). *Turning the world upside down: The search for global health in the twenty-first century*. London: Royal Society of medicine Press.

De Zwart, F. (2000). Personnel transfer in Indian state bureaucracy: Corruption and anti-corruption. In H. Bakker, & N. Nordholt (Eds.), *Corruption and legitimacy* (pp. 53–65). Amsterdam: Siswo.

Department for International Development. (2011). DFID's operational plan Uganda 2011–2015 at https://www.gov.uk/government/uploads/system/ uploads/attachment_data/file/67416/uganda-2011.pdf.

Dieleman, M., Toonen, J., Toure, H., & Martineau, T. (2006). The match between motivation and performance management of health sector workers in Mali. *Human Resources for Health, 4*, 2.

Ferro, A. (2006). Desired mobility or satisfied immobility? Migratory aspirations among knowledge workers. *Journal of Education and Work, 19*(2), 171–200.

Filippi, V., Ronsmans, C., Gohou, V., Goufodji, S., Lardi, M., Sahel, A., Saizonou, J., & De Brouwere, V. (2005). Maternal wards or emergency obstetric rooms? Incidence of near-miss events in African hospitals. *Acta Obstet Gynecol Scand, 84,* 11–16.

Franco, L.M., Bennett, S., & Kanfer, R. (2002). Health sector reform and public sector health worker motivation: A conceptual framework. *Social Science and Medicine, 54,* 1255–126.

Garcia-Prado, A., & Chawla, M. (2006). The impact of hospital management reforms on absenteeism in Cost Rica. *Health Policy and Planning, 21*(2), 91–100.

Gebauer, H., Worch, H., & Truffer, B. (2012). Absorptive capacity, learning processes and combinative capabilities as determinants of strategic innovation. *European Management Journal, 30,* 57–73.

General Medical Council. (2015). Good medical practice guide.

Gilson, L., Hanson, K., Sheikh, K., Agyepong, I.A., Ssengooba, F., & Bennett, S. (2011). Building the field of health policy and systems research: Social science matters. *PLoS Medicine, 8*(8), 1–6. www.plosmedicineorg.

Gluckler, J., Meusburger, P., & Meskioui, M.E. (2013). Introduction: Knowledge and the geography of the economy. In P. Meusburger, J. Gluckler, & M. Meskioui (Eds.), *Knowledge and the economy.* London: Springer.

Hallberg, I.R. (2015). Knowledge for health care practice. In D.A. Richards, & I.R. Hallberg (Eds.), *Complex interventions in health* (pp. 16–28). London: Routledge.

Harding, S. (Ed.). (1987). *Feminism and methodology.* Bloomington, IN: Indiana University Press.

Harding, S. (1991). *Whose science whose knowledge?* Ithaca: Cornell Press.

Helfat, E.C., & Peteraf, M.A. (2009). Understanding dynamic capabilities: Progress along a development path. *Strategic Organisation, 7*(1), 91–103.

House of Commons Committee of Public Accounts. (2016). Department for International Development: Responding to crisis, 35th Report of Session 2015–16.

HSCIC (2014). NHS workforce: Summary of staff in the NHS: results from September 2014 census. Health and Social Care Information Centre. http://www.hscic.gov.uk/.

Hudson, S., & Inkson, K. (2006). Volunteer overseas development workers: The hero's adventure and personal transformation. *Career Development International, 11*(4), 304–320.

Hurwitz, B. (1997). Swearing to care: The resurgence in medical oaths. *British Medical Journal, 315,* 1671.

Iyer, A., Sen, G., & Sreevathsa, A. (2013). Deciphering Rashomon: An approach to verbal autopsies of maternal deaths. *Global Public Health, 8*(4), 389–404.

James, J., Minett, C., & Ollier, L. (2008). *Evaluation of links between North and South healthcare organisations.* London: DFID Health Resource Centre.

Jones, B.D. (1999). Bounded rationality. *Annual Review of Political Science, 2,* 297–321.

Jones, F.A.E., Knights, D.P.H., Sinclair, V.F.E., & Baraitser, P. (2013). Do health partnerships with organisations in lower income countries benefit the UK partner? A review of the literature. *Globalisation and Health, 9*(38). http://www.globalizationandhealth.com/content/9/1/38.

Kaye, D.K., Kakaire, O., & Osinde, M.O. (2011). Maternal morbidity and near-miss mortality among women referred for emergency obstetric care in rural Uganda. *International Journal of Gynaecology and Obstetrics, 114,* 76–88.

Kesselring, S. (2006). Pioneering mobilities: New patterns of movement and motility in a mobile world. *Environment and Planning, 38,* 269–279.

Khan, A.S., & Ackers, P.B.H. (2004). Neo-pluralism as a theoretical framework for understanding HRM in sub-Saharan Africa. *International Journal of Human resource Management, 15*(7), 1330–1353.

Kinfu, Y., Dal Oz, M.R., Mercer, H., & Evans, D.B. (2009). The health worker shortage in Africa: Are enough physicians and nurses being trained? *Bulletin of the World Health Organisation, 87,* 225–230.

King, R. (2002). Towards a new map of European migration. *International Journal of Population Geography, 8*(2), 89–106.

Kuvic, A. (2015). The global competition for talent: Life science and biotech careers, international mobility and competitiveness. Unpublished PhD thesis. Department of Sociology, University of Amsterdam.

Liverpool School of Tropical Medicine. (2015). Maternal and neonatal health human resource capacity building, making it happen program annual review 2014 (unpublished).

Malecki, E.J. (2013). Creativity: Who, How, Where?.... In P. Meusberger, J. Gluckler, & M. Meskioui (Eds.), *Knowledge and the economy.* London: Springer.

Mangham, L.J., & Hanson, K. (2008). Employment preferences of public sector nurses in Malawi: Results from a discrete choice experiment. *Tropical Medicine and International Health, 13*(12), 1433–1441.

Marshall, T.H. (1950). *Citizenship and social class and other essays.* Cambridge, UK: Cambridge University Press.

Mathauer, I., & Imhoff, I. (2006). Health worker motivation in Africa: The role of non-financial incentives and human resource management tools. *Human Resources for Health, 4*(24). http://www.human-resources-health.com/content/4/1/24.

Mayer, R.E. (2008). *Learning and instruction.* Upper Saddle River, New Jersey: Pearson Education.

Mbindyo, P., Gilson, L., Blaauw, D., & English, M. (2009). Contextual influences on health worker motivation in district hospitals in Kenya. *Implementation Science, 4*(43). http://www.implementationscience.com/content/4/1/43.

McCormack, B. (2015). Action research for the implementation of complex interventions. In D.A. Richards, & I.R. Hallberg (Eds.), *Complex interventions in health* (pp. 300–311). London: Routledge.

McKay, A., & Ackers, H.L. (2013). SVP Benchmarking Report. Available at www.liverpoolmulagopartnership.org.

Meara, J.G., et al. (2015). Global surgery 2030: Evidence and solutions for achieving health, welfare, and economic development, Lancet commission report on global surgery. *Lancet, 386,* 569–624.

Medical Research Council. (2008). *Developing and evaluating complex interventions: New guidance.* London: Medical Research Council.

Meusberger, P. (2009). Spatial mobility of knowledge: A proposal for a more realistic communication model. *The Planning Review, 177*(2), 29–39.

Meusburger, P. (2013). Relations between knowledge and economic development: Some methodological considerations. In P. Meusburger, J. Gluckler, & M. Meskioui (Eds.), *Knowledge and the economy* (pp. 15–42). London: Springer.

Michie, S., Fixsen, D., Grimshaw, J.M., & Eccles, M.P. (2009). Specifying and reporting complex behaviour change interventions: The need for a scientific method. *Implementation Science, 4*(40). http://www.implementationscience.com/content/4/1/40.

Michie, S., Van Stralen, M.M., & West, R. (2011). The behaviour change wheel: A new method for characterising and designing behaviour change interventions. *Implementation Science, 6*(42). http://www.implementationscience.com/content/6/1/42.

Ministry of Health, Uganda. (2010). The Health Sector Strategic Plan III (2010/11-2014/15).

Ministry of Health, Uganda. (2015). Annual Health Sector Performance Report, Financial Year 2014/2015.

Moore, P., & Surgenor, M. (2012). The Ugandan maternal and newborn hub sustainable volunteering programme risk analysis July 2012. University Hospital of South Manchester NHS Foundation Trust.

Moyo, D. (2009). *Dead aid. Why aid is not working and how there is another way for Africa.* London: Penguin.

Muñoz, F.F., Encinar, M.I., & Canibano, C. (2011). On the role of intentionality in evolutionary economic change. *Structural Change and Economic Dynamics, 22,* 193–203.

Muñoz, F.F., & Encinar, M.I. (2014a). Agents intentionality, capabilities and the performance of systems of innovation. *Innovation: Management, Policy and Practice, 16*(1), 71–81.

Muñoz, F.F., & Encinar, M.I. (2014b). Intentionality and the emergence of complexity: An analytical approach. *Journal of Evolutionary Economics, 24,* 317–334.

Nzinga, J., Mbindyo, P., Mbaabu, L., Warira, A., & English, M. (2009). Documenting the experiences of health workers expected to implement guidelines during an intervention study in Kenyan hospitals. *Implementation Science*, 4(44). http://www.implementationscience.com/content/4/1/44.

Pacagnella, R.C., Cecatti, J.G., Osis, M.J., & Souza, J.P. (2012). The role of delays in severe maternal morbidity and mortality: Expanding the conceptual framework. *Reproductive Health Matters*, 20(39), 155–163.

Pfister, T. (2012). Citizenship and capability? Amartya Sen's capabilities approach from a citizenship perspective. *Citizenship Studies*, 16(2), 241–254.

Polanyi, M. (1959). *The study of man*. Chicago: Chicago University Press.

Richards, D.A. (2015). The complex interventions framework. In D.A. Richards, & I.R. Hallberg (Eds.), *Complex interventions in health* (pp. 1–15). London: Routledge.

Schaaf, M., & Freedman, L.P. (2015). Unmasking the open secret of posting and transfer practices in the health sector. *Health Policy and Planning*, 30, 121–130.

Sen, A. (1999). *Development as freedom*. Oxford: Oxford University Press.

Shrum, W.M., Duque, R.B., & Ynalvez, M.A. (2010). Outer space of science: A video ethnography of reagency in Ghana. In P. Meusburger, D.N. Livingstone, & H. Jons (Eds.), *Geographies of science* (pp. 151–165). Heidelberg: Springer.

Simon, H.A. (1985). Human nature in politics: The dialogue of psychology with political science. *American Political Science Review*, 79, 293–304.

Somekh, B. 2006. *Action research: A methodology for change and development*. Maidenhead: Open University Press.

Stringhini, S., Thomas, S., Bidwell, P., Mtui, T., & Mwisongo, A. (2009). Understanding informal payments in health care: Motivation of health workers in Tanzania. *Human Resources for Health*, 7(53). http://www.human-resources-health.com/content/7/1/53.

Tate, N. (2014). Emergency obstetric skills training. SVP Policy Report at www.knowledge4change.org.uk.

Tate, N. (2016). Investigating the experiences of doctors as volunteers in Uganda and the potential tensions that arise when attempting to create 'sustainable' change through voluntary placements. Unpublished Masters Dissertation.

Taylor, P.J., Hoyler, M., & Evans, D.M. (2013). A geohistorical study of "the rise of modern science": Mapping scientific practice through urban networks, 1500–1900. In P. Meusburger, D.N. Livingstone, & H. Jones (Eds.), *Geographies of science* (pp. 37–56). Heidelberg: Springer.

Teece, D., Psiano, G., & Shuen, A. (2000). Dynamic capabilities and strategic management. *Strategic Management Journals*, 18(7), 509–533.

Thaddeus, S., & Maine, D. (1990). *Too far to walk: Maternal mortality in context*. New York: Centre for population and family health, Colombia University School of Public Health.

Thorsen, V. C., Sundby, J., & Malata, A. (2012). Piecing together the maternal death puzzle through narrative: The three delays model revisited. *Plos One*, *7*(12), e52090.

Tropical Health Education Trust (THET). (2011). HPS volunteering grant: Concept paper guidelines. http://www.thet.org/hps/files/110919GCHPSVolunteeringGrantconceptguidelines.pdf.

Tropical Health Education Trust (THET). (2015). Putting Health workers at the heart of healthcare. http://www.thet.org/our-work/what-we-do.

Tropical Health Education Trust (THET). (2016). Health Partnership Scheme: Education and Training Reporting FAQ (sent to all project managers).

Tuncalp, O., Hindin, M.J., Souza, J.P., Chou, D., & Say, L. (2012). The prevalence of maternal near miss: A systematic review. *Bjog*, *119*, 653–661.

Uganda National Infection Prevention and Control Guidelines 2013, Ministry of Health, Uganda. (2014). Guidance on hand hygiene. http://library.health.go.ug/publications/leadership-and-governance-governance/guidelines/uganda-national-infection-prevention.

United Nations. (2013). Millennium development goals report for Uganda 2013. United Nationals Development Plan.

United Nations. (2015). Transforming our world: The 2030 Agenda for Sustainable Development.

Valters, C. (2015). Four Principles for theories of change in global development at www.odi.org/comment/9882-four-prinicples-theories-change-global-development.

Vian, T., Miller, C., Themba, Z., & Bukuluki, P. (2013). Perceptions of per diems in the health sector: Evidence and implications. *Health Policy and Planning*, *28*, 237–246.

West, R. (2006). Outline of a synthetic theory of addiction. on PRIME Theory of motivation website. http://www.primetheory.com/.

Williams, A. (2006). Lost in translation? International migration, learning and knowledge. *Progress in Human Geography*, *30*(5), 588–607.

Williams, A., & Balatz, V. (2008a). International return mobility, learning and knowledge transfer: A case study of Slovak doctors. *Social Science and Medicine*, *67*, 1924–1933.

Williams, A.M., & Balaz, V. (2008b). *International migration and knowledge*. London: Routledge.

Willis-Shattuck, M., Bidwell, P., Thomas, S., Wyness, L., Blaauw, D., & Ditlopo, P. (2008). Motivation and retention of health workers in developing countries: A systematic review. *BMC Health Services Research*, *8*(247). http://www.biomedcentral.com/1472-6963/8/247.

Wilson, A. (2008). Punching our weight, British academy. The humanities and social sciences in public policy making. http://www.britac.ac.uk/policy/wilson/.

Witt, U. (2004). On the proper interpretation of 'evolution' in economics and its implications for production theory. *Journal of Economic Methodology*, *11*, 125–146.

World Bank. (2009). Fiscal space for health in Uganda.

World Health Organisation. (2006). World health report: Working together for health.

World Health Organisation. (2010). World health statistics.

# INDEX

© The Author(s) 2017                                                              169
H.L. Ackers, J. Ackers-Johnson, *Mobile Professional Voluntarism
and International Development*, DOI 10.1057/978-1-137-55833-6

Printed in the United States
By Bookmasters